The Black Panther Party

Recent Titles in
Guides to Subcultures and Countercultures

Guides to
Subcultures and
Countercultures

The Black Panther Party

A Guide to an American Subculture

Jamie J. Wilson

GREENWOOD™

An Imprint of ABC-CLIO, LLC
Santa Barbara, California • Denver, Colorado

Library of Congress Cataloging-in-Publication Data

Names: Wilson, Jamie Jaywann, author.
Title: The Black Panther Party : a guide to an American subculture / Jamie J. Wilson.
Description: Santa Barbara, California : Greenwood, An Imprint of ABC-CLIO, LLC., [2018] |
    Series: Guides to subcultures and countercultures | Includes bibliographical references
    and index. | Description based on print version record and CIP data provided by
    publisher; resource not viewed.
Identifiers: LCCN 2017051698 (print) | LCCN 2017053799 (ebook) | ISBN 9780313392542
    (ebook) | ISBN 9780313392535 (hardcopy : alk. paper)
Subjects: LCSH: Black Panther Party—History. | African Americans—Politics and government—
    20th century. | African Americans—Civil rights—History—20th century. | Civil rights
    movements—United States—History—20th century. | United States—Race relations—History
    —20th century.
Classification: LCC E185.615 (ebook) | LCC E185.615 .W543 2018 (print) |
    DDC 322.4/20973—dc23
LC record available at https://lccn.loc.gov/2017051698

ISBN: 978-0-313-39253-5 (print)
      978-0-313-39254-2 (ebook)

22 21 20 19 18   1 2 3 4 5

This book is also available as an eBook.

Greenwood
An Imprint of ABC-CLIO, LLC

ABC-CLIO, LLC
130 Cremona Drive, P.O. Box 1911
Santa Barbara, California 93116-1911
www.abc-clio.com

This book is printed on acid-free paper ∞

Manufactured in the United States of America

Contents

Series Foreword

From Beatniks to Flappers, Zoot Suiters to Punks, this series brings to life some of the most compelling counterculture in American history. Designed to offer a quick in-depth examination and current perspective on each group, the series aims to stimulate the reader's understanding of the richness of the American experience. Each book explores a countercultural group critical to American life and introduces the reader to his or her historical setting and precedents, the ways in which it was subversive or countercultural, and its significance, and legacy in American history. *Webster's Ninth New Collegiate Dictionary* defines "counterculture" as "a culture and values and mores that run counter to those of established society." Although some of the groups covered can be described as primarily subcultural, they were targeted for inclusion because they have not existed in a vacuum. They have advocated for rules that methodically opposed mainstream culture, or they have lived by their ideals to the degree that it became impossible not to impact the society around them. They have left their marks, both positive and negative, on the fabric of American culture. Volumes cover such groups as Hippies and Beatniks, who impacted popular culture, literature, and art; the eco-socialists and radical feminists, who worked toward social and political change; and even groups such as the Ku Klux Klan, who left mostly scars.

A lively alternative to narrow historiography and scholarly monographs, each volume in the *Subcultures and Countercultures* series can be described as a "library in a book," containing both essays and browsable reference materials, including primary documents, to enhance the research process and bring the content alive in a variety of ways. Written for students and general readers, each volume includes engaging illustrations, a timeline of critical events in the subculture, topical essays that illuminate aspects of the subculture, a glossary of terms and slangs, biographical sketches of the key players involved, and primary source excerpts—including speeches, writings, articles, first-person accounts, memoirs, diaries, government reports, and court decisions—that offer contemporary perspective on each group. In addition, each volume includes an extensive bibliography of recommended print and nonprint sources appropriate for research.

Preface

The Black Panther Party (BPP) was a popular African American political organization during the Black Power movement of the late 1960s and early 1970s. Huey P. Newton and Bobby Seale, the founders of the organization, initially named the organization the Black Panther Party for Self Defense and Justice, but later shortened the name to the Black Panther Party. From the outset, according to historians Joshua Bloom and Waldo Martin, authors of *Black against Empire: The History and Politics of the Black Panther Party*: "[the] Black Panther Party rejected the legitimacy of the U.S. government. The Panthers saw black communities in the United States as a colony and the police as an occupying army."[1]

During their period of activism, white America largely ignored socioeconomic problems in urban African American communities even while black bodies were beaten by the hands of white police and black lives were cut down by police bullets. In the face of such violence, African American civil rights organizations like the National Association for the Advancement of Colored People (NAACP), the National Urban League (NUL), the Congress of Racial Equality (CORE), and the Student Nonviolent Coordinating Committee (SNCC) opposed police brutality, but did not provide national strategies, mechanisms, or challenges to daily police brutality in black communities. Even black separatist groups like the Nation of Islam (NOI), an influential African American Islamic organization known for its contempt of the United States and its hatred of white America, as well as its rehabilitative work among poor and working-class African Americans, did not propose armed self-defense in black communities.

The BPP did. Like its ideological predecessor, the Deacons for Self Defense, a southern African American civil rights group, the BPP espoused a strategy of armed self-defense. In a political environment and time when African Americans' tactics of direct, nonviolent action and legal challenges were seen as the most effective ways to bring about racial justice, BPP's confrontational style and critiques of local law enforcement throughout the nation defied civil rights orthodoxy and white authority.

The BPP's community survival programs also challenged the economic status quo. Public schools provide free breakfast for low-income children throughout the nation now, but in the late 1960s and early 1970s, they did not. Administrators and policy makers on the federal and local levels turned a blind eye to hunger, so the BPP fed thousands of black and white children weekly at the height of its free breakfast program. Yohuru Williams, the historian and author of several books about the BPP, has noted that "[t]he Free Breakfast for Schoolchildren Program enlisted Panthers every day in dozens of cities across the country and became a blueprint for the federal government's school breakfast and lunch program."[2] In so doing, it challenged the common narrative that hunger in African American communities was the result of African Americans' unwillingness to work and that poverty was a consequence of the inherent moral failings of the black poor; instead, hunger was a result of a fundamentally flawed economic system and a racial hierarchy that created and maintained black ghettos. American consumer capitalism was the problem. According to the BPP, it was a flawed economic system that exploited black people and other people of color. Despite Cold War fears of leftist movements and ideologies, the BPP argued that socialism would be an equitable economic and political system for African Americans and the vast majority of Americans.

Over the last 50 years, scholars, activists, journalists, and critics have written many articles and monographs about the Black Panther

part. Within the last decade, there has been a renewed scholarly interest in the organization that moves beyond intellectual and political
posturing and toward a fuller historical understanding of the group's
contribution to the African American freedom struggle. Most of these
studies have recognized the importance and influence of the Central
Committee and the party's founding Oakland, California, chapter
and focus on BPP chapters and affiliates in cities throughout the
nation. Together, they argue that each local entity of the party was
shaped by and responded to the specific needs and concerns of the
African American communities it served. This book takes this
approach by looking at the BPP in various cities throughout the
nation. At its zenith, the party had 68 recognized chapters and affiliates, but there were also groups that claimed to be Black Panthers
and were not officially associated with the group. As an introduction
to the BPP, this study does not seek to tell the stories of all the local
chapters, branches, and affiliates; to do so would be impossible. However, it does highlight and discuss some of the most important developments of and challenges for the BPP throughout the nation,
paying attention to the local realities.

Chapter one situates the BPP within the shifting political terrain of
the African American freedom struggle of the late 1960s and early 1970s.
It examines political influences on the party, the party's early development, and some of the ways it influenced other political activists.
Chapter two discusses Black Panthers in the American South. Conven-
tional historical thinking for those unfamiliar with African American
history problematically assumes that racial injustice disappeared when
the modern United States civil rights movement achieved major judicial
victories and concluded throughout southern states. The reality is that
African Americans continued to face structural racism in the late 1960s
and early 1970s. The BPP in at least three southern cities—Houston,
Texas; New Orleans, Louisiana; and Winston-Salem, North Carolina
—worked with local black communities to challenge those forces that
kept them poor, undereducated, underemployed, and segregated.

Chapter three examines BPP activity in the northeastern section
of the United States giving attention to Boston and New Bedford,
Massachusetts, and New Haven, Connecticut. Events that unfolded
in New Haven made that chapter one of the most dramatic and compelling in BPP history. Chapter four looks at Black Panthers in cities

in America's north central states, which had African American populations of varying sizes. Chapter five considers the ways in which the BPP have been depicted in popular culture including films and hip-hop culture. The book closes with a discussion of the legacy of the party.

Notes

1. Joshua Bloom and Waldo E. Martin Jr., *Black against Empire: The History and Politics of the Black Panther Party* (Berkeley: University of California Press, 2013), 2.
2. Bryan Shih and Yohuru Williams, *The Black Panthers: Portraits from an Unfinished Revolution* (New York: Nation Books, 2016), 50.

Acknowledgments

Sincere gratitude and appreciation to my dear wife, Staci, for her support, edits, and patience with me as I worked on this project. When books and papers were piled high and scattered, she let me slide. Many thanks to Michael Millman and the entire ABC-CLIO family for working with me and giving the chance to write about such an important topic.

Finally, as ever, I am thankful to all my ancestors, known and unknown, who allowed me this opportunity.

Acronyms and Abbreviations

BPP or Panthers	Black Panther Party
COINTELPRO	Counterintelligence Program
DSD	Deacons for Self Defense
FBI	Federal Bureau of Investigation
FBIS	Foreign Broadcast Information Service
MMI	Muslim Mosque Incorporated
NAACP	National Association for the Advancement of Colored People
NBPP	New Black Panther Party
NCCF	National Committee to Combat Fascism
NHPDC	New Haven Panther Defense Committee
NOI	The Nation of Islam
OAAU	Organization of African American Unity
OBSU	Organization of Black Student Unity
OCS	Oakland Community School
PFMC	People's Free Medical Clinic
PP II	People's Party II
RNA	Republic of New Afrika

SAC	Special Agent in Charge
SDS	Students for a Democratic Society
SNCC	Student Nonviolent Coordinating Committee
UCLA	University of California, Los Angeles
UNIA	Universal Negro Improvement Association

Timeline

October 1966   Huey P. Newton and Bobby Seale organize the Black Panther Party.

April 28, 1967   Muhammad Ali refuses to be inducted into the U.S. Army. He convicted of draft evasion, stripped of his heavyweight title, and banned from boxing. His conviction was overturned in 1970. Ali would go on to win the heavy title again in 1974.

May   The Black Panther Party publicizes its Ten Point Program.

May 2   Bobby Seale leads a group of 32 armed Panthers to Sacramento, California, the state capitol, to protest the Mulford Act, a statute that outlawed carrying loaded weapons in public spaces. Seale read Executive Mandate No. 1. It declared that "The Black Panther Party for Self-defense believes that the time has come for black people to arm themselves against this terror before it is too late."

June 12   The U.S. Supreme Court unanimously decides *Loving v. Virginia*. The case legalized interracial marriage throughout the nation.

June 29   Huey P. Newton delivers his Executive Mandate No. 2. It officially recognized Stokely Carmichael, the former chairman of the Student Nonviolent Coordinating Committee, as a "Field Marshal." Carmichael was given the authority to "to establish revolutionary law, order and justice in the territory lying between the Continental Divide East to the Atlantic Ocean, North of the Mason-Dixon Line to the Canadian Border, South of the Mason-Dixon Line to the Gulf of Mexico."

July 12–17   Race riots erupt in Newark, New Jersey.

July 17   John Coltrane dies. Coltrane was one of the greatest jazz saxophonists of the 20th century and genius behind the 1965 album *A Love Supreme*.

July 23–30   Race riots erupt in Detroit, Michigan.

August 25   Director of the Federal Bureau of Investigation (FBI), J. Edgar Hoover, releases a memo instructing FBI agents around the nation to formulate and execute counterintelligence measures to neutralize and disable party chapters throughout the nation.

August 30   Thurgood Marshall is confirmed by the U.S. Senate and becomes the first African American Supreme Court Justice.

September 12   Stokely Carmichael publishes *Black Power: The Politics of Liberation* with sociologist Charles Hamilton.

1968   Workers, activists, and intellectuals create the Dodge Revolutionary Union Movement to correct problems in Detroit's automobile industry.

James Brown releases *Say It Loud, I'm Black and I'm Proud*.

February   Eldridge Cleaver's *Soul on Ice* is published.

	The Student Nonviolent Coordinating Committee and the Black Panther Party merge. The merger is a brief one.
February 25	Berkeley, California, police raid Bobby Seale's apartment without a warrant and charge him with conspiracy to commit murder. The charges were eventually dropped.
March 1	Huey P. Newton issues Executive Mandate No. 3. The decree maintained that "all members must acquire the technical equipment to defend their homes and their dependents."
April 4	Martin Luther King Jr. is assassinated. After the announcement of his death, violence erupts in inner cities throughout the nation.
April 6	Bobby Hutton, one of the original members of the Black Panther Party, is killed in an altercation with the Oakland Police Department.
May 14	Eldridge Cleaver, minister of information for the BPP, becomes the presidential nominee for the Peace and Freedom Party.
September 8	Huey P. Newton is found guilty of the manslaughter in the death of Patrolman John Frey.
October	Tommie Smith, gold medalist, and John Carlos, bronze medalist, in the 200-meter race, raise clenched fists in the black power salute during the Olympic medal ceremony. The two were expelled from the Olympic Games.
November 5	Shirley Chisholm is the first African American woman elected to Congress.
December 18	Local police and FBI agents raid the Indianapolis, Indiana, Black Panther Party office ostensibly looking for a cache of weapons. No weapons were found.
1969	James Foreman publishes his "Black Manifesto," calling on white churches and synagogues to pay

black people reparations for generations of exploitation.

Dial Press releases *Die Nigger Die!*, H. Rap Brown's autobiography. Brown was chairman of the Student Nonviolent Coordinating Committee and a member of the Black Panther Party.

January	The first free breakfast for children program begins at the St. Augustine Episcopal Church in West Oakland, California.
January 17	John Huggins is killed by members of Ron Karenga's US organization on the University of California, Los Angeles, campus.
January 22	The Third World Liberation Front, a multiethnic student organization, begins its strike at the University of California, Berkeley. The strike lasted for several weeks.
April 1	The Chicago chapter of the Black Panther Party opens its free breakfast for children program.
June 4	The FBI raid Black Panthers headquarters in Chicago, Illinois.
July 18-21	Black Panthers hold the United Front against Fascism Conference in Oakland, California.
July 31	Chicago police raid Black Panthers headquarters in Chicago, Illinois.
August 9	Richmond, California, police unsuccessfully attempt to evict panthers from their local office.
August 15	Sylvester Bell, a member of the San Diego, California Black Panther Party, is killed by members of Ron Karenga's US organization.
September	After a rally against the Vietnam War at the 1968 Democratic Convention in Chicago, Illinois, Bobby Seale is arrested and detained. During court appearance, he is shackled and gagged as per the judge's order.

September 2	San Diego police destroy the local Panthers' office allegedly in search of a suspected murderer.
September 23	Philadelphia, Pennsylvania, police, along with FBI agents, arrest members of the local Philadelphia chapter in their office.
October 4	Chicago police raid Black Panther Party headquarters in Chicago, Illinois, the third raid in three months.
November 13	Spurgeon Jake Winters, a Black Panther in Chicago, Illinois, kills a police officer in a shoot-out. After a short manhunt, he is killed by police.
December 4	Fred Hampton, leader of the Chicago Black Panther Party, is killed by the Chicago Police Department.
December 8	Los Angeles police raid Black Panthers' offices.
1970	Bobby Seale, the chairman of the Black Panther Party, publishes *Seize the Time: The Story of the Black Panther Party and Huey P. Newton.*
	Lee Lockwood publishes *Conversation with Eldridge Cleaver.*
	Maya Angelou publishes *I Know Why the Caged Bird Sings.*
	The Omaha, Nebraska, chapter is expelled from the BPP.
	The Franklin Lynch People's Free Medical Clinic opens in Boston, Massachusetts.
January 14	New York City Black Panthers raise $10,000 during a fund-raiser at the home of Leonard Bernstein, the conductor of the New York Philharmonic.
March 8	The Black Panthers' office in Philadelphia, Pennsylvania, is incinerated after an unknown suspect tossed a bomb through a window.
May 29	Huey P. Newton's conviction of manslaughter is overturned by the California Appellate Court.

June 29	The Cleveland, Ohio, Police Department raids the local Black Panther Party headquarters allegedly to serve an arrest warrant.
July	The FBI names the Black Panther Party "the most dangerous and violence prone of all extremist groups."
	A branch of the National Committee to Combat Fascism is created in New Bedford, Massachusetts.
July 14	Eldridge Cleaver, Elaine Brown, and other members of progressive political organizations arrive in Pyongyang, North Korea, as official North Korean guests to discuss anti-imperialism throughout the world.
July 26	Carl Hampton, a member of People's Party II, a Black Panther Party affiliate in Houston, Texas, is shot and killed by police.
July 31	New Bedford, Massachusetts, police raid the National Committee to Combat Fascism headquarters.
August 5	Huey P. Newton is released from prison.
	Police Officer Larry Minard of the Omaha, Nebraska, Police Department is killed by a bomb planted by Duane Peak, a teenager and member of the Omaha National Committee to Combat Fascism.
August 31	Police in Philadelphia, Pennsylvania, raid three BPP office in hopes of finding suspects connected with the shooting of police officers.
September 5–7	The Black Panther Party's Revolutionary People's Constitutional Convention meets in Philadelphia, Pennsylvania.
September 15	Officers of the New Orleans Police Department raid the National Committee to Combat Fascism headquarters in city's Ninth Ward, ostensibly to serve a warrant for arrest.

October 2	Des Moines, Iowa, police raid the local Black Panther Party headquarters.
October 24-25	The Detroit, Michigan, Black Panther Party headquarters is raided by Detroit police.
November 18	Huey P. Newton speaks to hundreds of students, activists, and intellectuals at the Rogers Center at Boston University in Boston, Massachusetts.
November 26	Officers of the New Orleans Police Department dressed as priests and maintenance workers raid the New Orleans's National Committee to Combat Fascism apartment in the Desire Housing Project in the city's Ninth Ward.
1971	Gil Scott Heron releases his album, *The Revolution Will Not Be Televised*, on the Flying Dutchman label. The Last Poets release their album *This Is Madness* for Douglass Music. The albums put to music the frustrations and anguish felt by African Americans throughout the nation.
	Reverend Jesse Jackson establishes People United to Save Humanity in Chicago, Illinois.
	Film director John Evans releases *Huey P. Newton: Prelude to Revolution*.
	Film director Howard Alk releases *The Murder of Fred Hampton*.
February	Huey P. Newton expels Eldridge Cleaver and the International Section from the Black Panther Party.
April 2	Jersey City police raid the Black Panther Party office in Jersey City, New Jersey.
May 12	After a 13-month trial, the New York 21, 21 Black Panthers in New York City are found not guilty by a jury of their peers. One hundred and fifty-six not guilty verdicts were given on a variety of charges including but not limited to terrorism charges.
May 21	Marvin Gaye releases *What's Goin' On*. In 2003, *Rolling Stone* named *What's Goin' On* one of the

	top 500 albums of all times. The album encapsulates the rhythm and blues and soul music in African American culture of the era.
May 25	Judge Harold Mulvey declares a mistrial in the cases of Bobby Seale and Ericka Huggins. Seale and Huggins were accused of participating in the murder of Alex Rackley in New Haven, Connecticut.
July	The Chicago-based rhythm and blues singing sensation, The Chi-Lites, release "(For God's Sake) Give More Power to the People."
August 21	George Jackson, Black Panther Party member and author, is killed by guards at San Quentin State Prison in Marin County, California.
September 9	Prisoners at Attica Correctional facility in New York State take control of the prison. Several days later, on September 13, state police retook the prison, killing 39 people.
March 10, 1972	The National Black Political Assembly convenes on March 10, 1972, in Gary, Indiana. Black intellectuals, elected politicians, and activists meet to consider the most appropriate strategies to free black people from the chains of generational discrimination, economic poverty, and electoral neglect.
May 20	The Central Committee in Oakland, California, announces that Bobby Seale would run for mayor of Oakland.
June	Angela Davis, the African American feminist intellectual and member of the Communist Party, is acquitted and released from prison.
July	Huey P. Newton calls for chapters throughout the country to consolidate in Oakland, California, to support Bobby Seale's mayoral campaign.
1973	Huey P. Newton publishes his autobiography, *Revolutionary Suicide*.

August	After being expelled from the party in 1969, a chapter of the Black Panther Party is reconstituted in Milwaukee, Wisconsin.
September	The first class of students begin school at the Oakland Community School, a school operated by the Black Panther Party.
June 1974	Activist and intellectuals participate in the Sixth Pan African Conference in Dar es Salaam, Tanzania.
July	Huey P. Newton expels Bobby Seale from the party.
	Elaine Brown becomes chairwoman of the Black Panther Party.
August	Huey P. Newton is accused of murder, flees the United States, and takes up residence in Cuba.
1975	The funk band Parliament releases *Chocolate City*. In its title track, the album imagines the United States if African Americans were in charge of the White House.
1977	Huey P. Newton returns to the United States and reclaims control of the Black Panther Party. He is put on trial and eventually has his murder charges dismissed. Party membership hovers around 200.
1982	Elaine Brown publishes her memoir *A Taste of Power: A Black Woman's Story*.
1989	Dedicating itself to "revolutionary organization with an Afrikan-centered ideology," the New Black Panther Party is founded in Dallas, Texas.
August 22	Huey P. Newton is murdered in West Oakland, California.
1995	Director Melvin Van Peebles releases *Panther*, the first feature length dramatization of the Black Panther Party.
1996	Harlem River Press publishes Huey P. Newton's *War against The Panthers: A Study of Repression in America*. The book is a revision of his doctoral thesis at the University of California, Santa Cruz.

1998   Xenon Video, Inc., releases an extensive interview with then imprisoned Huey P. Newton, circa 1971.

2014   The Huey P. Newton Foundation, a nonprofit organization created by former Black Panther Party members, denounces the New Black Panther Party.

2015   Film director Stanley Nelson releases the documentary *The Black Panthers: Vanguard of the Revolution*. To date, it is the most well-researched and balanced documentary of the Black Panther Party.

CHAPTER ONE

All Power to the
People: Black
Power Politics
after the Civil
Rights Movement

The Black Panther Party (BPP or Panthers) must be understood within the changing context of African American political struggles in the late 1960s and early 1970s. The phrase "black power" was popularized in 1966 by Stokely Carmichael during a civil rights march in Mississippi.[1] Since its first utterance, "black power" has become an amorphous term and was conceptualized differently by many of its most vocal adherents and activists. However, for the purposes of this chapter and discussion, "black power" is defined as African Americans' experimentation with democratic processes to bring about social, cultural, and political self-determination for the communities they lived in and served.[2] As the years between 1954 and 1966 represent the classical period of the modern civil rights movement, the period between 1966 and 1974 is the era commonly understood to be the zenith of Black Power politics. To be sure, African Americans' search for self-determination paralleled, overlapped, informed, and was informed by civil rights activists' attempts to achieve school integration, equal access in public accommodations, and voting rights. In fact, it was the civil rights movement's reforms that gave Black Power activists the courage to challenge persistent and growing economic and political inequalities. Historian Clarence Lang's comments about

Black Power activism in St. Louis, Missouri, can be applied to activists nationwide. He notes that "bitter experiences of arrests, beatings, church bombings, and assassinations" of John F. Kennedy, Medgar Evers, Malcolm X, Martin Luther King, Jr., Robert F. Kennedy, and countless other grassroots activists "helped to sour younger activists on the idea that they could end racism, poverty, and militarism through American liberalism."[3]

The Black Panther Party's Ideological Influences

Throughout the nation, though mainly focused in northeastern, midwestern, and western cities, Black Power advocates attempted to improve their communities, which, by the late 1960s, were all-black enclaves. In so doing, they exposed the contradictions between equal rights and equality of opportunity on the one hand, and continued racism and poverty on the other. Their approaches radicalized members of civil rights groups like Congress of Racial Equality and Student Nonviolent Coordinating Committee (SNCC) and spurred the creation of new black political organizations like the BPP. Unfortunately, some of their rhetoric and activism led to rivalries among and between organizations and conflicts between activists and law enforcement.

Historians are just beginning to understand and reconceptualize the complexities and extent of the Black Power movement. However, the notion that it was "consistent with preceding" black political efforts and reflected "continuity and change in the African American experience" in the decades following World War II is common knowledge among historians of the African American experience and merits our attention in any discussion of the black politics in the second half of the 20th century (Lang 2010, 68). What follows is a discussion of how Black Power political activists dreamed of black political freedom and strategized and worked to make that dream a reality. It explores the influential theorists, some of the most important Black Power organizations, and major campaigns.

Black power advocates and activists were unanimously influenced by Malcolm X. Born Malcolm Little on May 19, 1925, to Earl and Louisa Little in Omaha, Nebraska, Malcolm X, during his early years, was taught the black nationalist teachings of Marcus Garvey and the

Universal Negro Improvement Association (UNIA). With its head-quarters in Harlem, New York, and branches in towns and cities across the United States and throughout the world, the UNIA was the largest black mass movement in U.S. history. Garvey taught race pride, Pan-Africanism, black cooperative economics, and an anti-colonial message that would provide the basic ideological tenets of Malcolm's lifework as a Muslim minister. When Malcolm was six years old, his father died under mysterious circumstances when he was hit by a street car. Officially his death was ruled an accident, but the Little family believed Earl's death was the result of violence meted out by local white men who had repeatedly intimidated and assaulted the Little family. With his father gone, his mother struggled to keep her family together, but with too many mouths to feed, Malcolm was placed into foster care. Eventually, poverty and stress took its toll on his mother. In 1939, she was committed to the Kalamazoo State Hospital where she stayed for over two decades.

In 1941, Malcolm moved to Roxbury section of Boston, Massachusetts, to live with his half-sister Ella Collins (Earl's daughter from a previous marriage). In Boston, Malcolm became acquainted with jazz (a love of his for his entire adult life) and petty crime. At the age of 16, he obtained employment as a cook and later as a waiter on the railroad. Through his travels between Washington, D.C., and Boston, he frequented Harlem, New York, the black cultural capital of the United States. In the mid- to late 1940s, Malcolm made frequent trips between Boston and New York City and became more involved in crime, burglarizing homes in Boston's affluent suburbs. In January 1946, he and his friend in crime, Shorty Jarvis, were arrested; charged with firearm possession, larceny, and breaking and entering; and were sentenced to four concurrent sentences of eight to ten years each. During his time in prison at the Norfolk Prison Colony in Norfolk, Massachusetts, he converted to the Nation of Islam (NOI). The NOI is a heterodox, American Islamic movement in the United States founded in Detroit, Michigan, during the Great Depression by W. Fard Muhammad, a traveling peddler who declared that he was the messiah for black people. Throughout the 1940s, despite internal disputes and turmoil, the organization remained afloat under the leadership of Elijah Muhammad, a position he would hold until his death in 1975. In the spirit of Marcus Garvey, the NOI created black-owned businesses and taught black racial pride. It also restricted adherents from participating in partisan politics. More importantly, it offered its members, many of whom were ex-convicts and recovering drug addicts, a regimented life.

Malcolm was released from prison in 1952. After his parole ended in 1953, he traveled the country teaching the ideas and doctrines of Elijah Muhammad. In 1957, after several tireless years of work as the head minister of Temple No. 7 in Harlem and the principal organizer of temples throughout the eastern seaboard, his charisma and work brought him to the attention of Elijah Muhammad who promoted him to the position of national spokesman for the NOI. In 1958, Malcolm married Betty Shabazz (nee Sanders), a nurse and health instructor for NOI's Muslim Girl's Training General Civilization Class. During the late 1950s and early 1960s, Betty would give birth to six girls. It was also during these years that Malcolm continued to seek converts for the organization, hold rallies, speak at colleges and universities, travel to the Middle East to prepare the way for Elijah Muhammad's pilgrimage, write columns for black newspapers, and frame himself as a burgeoning civil rights leader. In 1959, he was featured in Mike Wallace's *The Hate That Hate Produced*, a documentary that unflatteringly introduced white Americans to the NOI's politics and leaders. By 1960, Malcolm was one of the most popular and hated black leaders in the NOI.

Malcolm's affiliation with the NOI changed on November 22, 1963, when John F. Kennedy was assassinated. Elijah Muhammad ordered that no minister or member of the NOI was to make a public statement about the death of the president. Despite this, when asked by a reporter what he thought about Kennedy's death, Malcolm commented that it was a case of "chickens coming home to roost," a statement for which he was suspended.[4] Knowing that he would not be reinstated to his position, on March 8, 1964, Malcolm announced that he would leave the NOI. Throughout the spring of 1964, he made plans to organize the Muslim Mosque Incorporated (MMI) for which he was the head minister.

The year 1964, the final year of Malcolm's short life, was a busy one. Shortly after organizing the MMI, he made a pilgrimage to Mecca, converted to Sunni Islam, and changed his name to El Hajj Malik el Shabazz. Upon his return to the United States, he denounced the heterodox views of his mentor Elijah Muhammad, exposed Muhammad's adulterous activity with female secretaries in the organization, and organized the Organization of Afro American Unity (OAAU) as a secular political wing for his civil rights works. In the fall of 1964, he set out on a tour of Africa to gain support from African heads of state and dignitaries for a UN resolution condemning institutional racism and segregation in the United States. His work during this year was a major shift in his approach. He was now willing to work with whites and blacks in the civil rights movement and place black people's fight against oppression on a world stage.

Malcolm X's fiery speaking style, his willingness to engage the most educated and uneducated listeners and debaters, his ability to distill complex ideas to their very essence, and his linking of African Americans' political struggle against racism with the anti-colonial struggles around the African diaspora are what so many Black Power activists found attractive and influential. For people who were victims of police brutality in urban areas, his call for self-defense was appealing. To the impoverished, his assessment of the causes of their poverty rang true. For young people looking for someone who could speak the language of the street, who was from the street, who understood the complexities of urban living, and who could offer an ideological and political alternative to Martin Luther King, Jr., Malcolm was an obvious choice. His work, however, was cut short when he was assassinated on February 21, 1965, while speaking at an OAAU rally at the Audubon Ballroom in Harlem, New York. His *Autobiography* was published posthumously in 1965 and, along with his speeches, was considered required reading by activists.[5]

Huey P. Newton and the BPP, like many other activists, were Malcolm X's ideological offspring. The BPP was founded in 1966 in Oakland, California, as an armed community police patrol by Huey P. Newton and Bobby Seale. Bobby Seale was the organization's chairman. Newton was the minister for self-defense and the group's chief political philosopher. In 1967, Eldridge Cleaver, the Left-leaning author of *Soul on Ice*, joined the organization and became the organization's minister of information.[6] The Panthers were influenced by Malcolm X's internationalist approach, the Martinican psychologist and author Frantz Fanon who argued that armed violence used by the colonized is necessary and can be cathartic, Marxist ideologies, and Mao Zedong, as well as local, national, and international radical politics including anti-colonial struggles in Latin America, Africa, and Asia. Newton guided the BPP toward black nationalism in its opening years and argued that black people possessed the right to control the politics, culture, and economies of their communities. Throughout its lifetime, the organization shifted its ideological position to socialism, and then intercommunalism. As intercommunalists, "the Panthers saw their struggle in the United States as not only necessary for the liberation of blacks and other oppressed people in America but as a struggle whose success was critical for the liberation of nations worldwide."[7] Intercommunalism as a political approach wed the complexities of empire building, western neo-imperialist projects and international grassroots mobilizations that were not limited by political geography.

Such an international perspective harkens back to W.E.B. Du Bois's Pan-African conferences between World War I and World War II, Marcus Garvey's Universal Negro Improvement Association of the 1920s, and the Council of African Affairs that sought to cultivate political ties across the African diaspora in the immediate post–World War II decade. With the emergence of the nonaligned movement in Bandung, Indonesia, in 1955 and as Asian, Latin American, and African nations broke the yoke of colonialism, black activists built on previous ideas of internationalism and individually, collectively, creatively, and strategically made political connections with and were inspired by people of color in other nations.

The Black Panther Party's Origins and Growth

The members of the BPP portrayed themselves as young revolutionaries known for their bellicose rhetoric and style. On May 2, 1967, a group of armed Panthers demonstrated at the Capitol Building in Sacramento, California, to decry legislation being considered that would criminalize the carrying of weapons. The demonstration gave the Panthers media attention throughout the country and brought the organization to the attention of both urban blacks seeking a political outlet and the Federal Bureau of Investigation (FBI). In early 1968, the party launched its weekly newspaper, *The Black Panther*, which had a circulation of over 100,000 at the height of its popularity. By 1970, four years after its creation and to the surprise of its founders, the party grew to over 5,000 members, divided into more than 40 chapters and affiliates nationwide.

Its growth is partially the result of the group's brief merger with SNCC in 1968. Both SNCC and the Panthers sought to use the other

H. Rap Brown, national chairperson of the Student Non-violent Coordinating Committee (SNCC) and a leader in the Black Power movement, during a press conference on July 27, 1967. SNCC and the BPP briefly joined forces in the late 1960s. Brown was shot and wounded in 1967 after delivering a fiery speech about the cause. The Black Power movement was an attempt by militant African Americans to establish their own political, cultural, and social institutions independent of white society. (Library of Congress)

to extend the reach of their work into new areas. SNCC wanted to reach out to blacks in urban locations and the Panthers wanted to help mobilize African Americans in the South. With SNCC's Stokely Carmichael as prime minster of the party, James Forman and H. Rap Brown became the minister of foreign affairs and minister of justice, respectively. The union failed not only because of mutual distrust, leadership difference, and FBI subterfuge, but also because both organizations were moving in opposing political directions, SNCC toward black nationalism and the Panthers closer to socialism.

As it emerged on the national scene, the BPP became one of the targets of the FBI's Counterintelligence Program (COINTELPRO). In conjunction with local police agencies, the bureau used a variety of techniques to destroy the organization including, but not limited to, spreading misinformation in media outlets, raiding local headquarters, and creating a culture of harassment. During an October 28, 1967, traffic stop, an altercation ensued between Officer John Frey, Officer Herbert Heanes, and Huey P. Newton. When the fracas was over, Frey lay dead. Heanes was hurt and Newton's body was riddled with bullets. The state accused Newton of murder and brought several other charges. At his trial on September 8, 1968, the court found him guilty of manslaughter and sentenced him 2 to 15 years at the California Men's Prison Colony in San Luis Obispo, California. After a series of retrials, Newton was exonerated and was released from prison in August 1970.

Around the country, local branches started running survival programs. Survival programs had three purposes. The first was the empowerment of African Americans, especially young people living in urban areas, through political education. The second purpose was to ensure the health and safety of poor, urban black communities within which the Panthers worked. The third was more far reaching. Through such initiatives, Panthers sought to break down exploitative economic relationships that made urban black people poor in the first place. Not all the chapters ran the same programs and different names were used depending on the location. Despite differences in program names, chapters throughout the country ran survival programs that included free breakfast programs for children, before- and after-school education programs, Free Busing to Prisons Program, Sickle Cell Anemia Research Program, and Seniors against Fearful Environment program, as well as household maintenance services.

By 1974, state chapters throughout the nation closed and nation-wide membership dwindled to around 500. During that year, Newton fled to Cuba to avoid imprisonment for the alleged murder of a prostitute and Elaine Brown became the party's chairwoman, who reversed many of Newton's policies and tried to save the crippled organization.[8] As head of the party and with the leadership of a cadre of black women whom she appointed, Brown opened and operated the Oakland Community School (OCS). The school became a beacon for public education and received several awards for its work. For example, Saturu Ned, a former teacher at the school, remembers a California legislature award ceremony from the 1970s during which the school was recognized for its educational successes. "Huey P. Newton stood up in front of them and somebody handed him a bouquet of flowers. I looked at one of the other guys. 'Can you believe this?' We brought national attention to the education aspect of the party."[9]

Newton had returned to the United States in 1977 to be cleared of all charges. From 1977 to 1982, he assumed leadership of the party. But, during this time, with close to 200 members, the party was a shadow of its former self. *The Black Panther* ceased publication in 1980 and the OCS closed its doors in 1982, the same year the party disbanded.

The Panthers' national profile and community programs often served as a model for other organizations around the county. The Liberators was one such group. A short-lived, male-dominated group of young activists in St Louis, Missouri, the Liberators was founded in 1968 by Charles Koen, a former member of SNCC who recruited members from rival gangs in the city. The Liberators organized a free breakfast program, donned berets and leather jackets like the San Francisco Bay Area Panthers, worked to end police brutality, and openly protested the drafting of black men into the military. It was the Panthers' willingness to experiment with the concept of black power that inspired other Black Power activists.

Creating Opportunities for Change: Convening Black Power

The multiplicity of interpretations of black power in the late 1960s led to a multifaceted grassroots approach that sought to improve employment opportunities, end segregated housing policies, and integrate

Huey P. Newton poses in Black Panther poster with a spear in one hand a shotgun in the other. (Library of Congress)

public accommodations. For some Black Power activists, "black power meant shoring up black manhood, advocating self-defense, seeking self-determination, exercising political power, attacking discrimination in education, employment, housing, and welfare, challenging entrenched white and black leaders, and mobilizing poor black people to transform society."[10]

Throughout the classical Black Power era, activists came together in several conferences and assemblies to discuss the meaning of black power in their communities and brainstorm about the future of black activism on a nationwide level. Black students and intellectuals met on college campuses, black radicals gathered in smoke-filled rooms and bars, and black bohemians assembled in cafes to discuss issues prior to a conference, but these meetings were often clandestine and held in isolation. What is significant about the conferences and assemblies which met in Newark, New Jersey (1967), Philadelphia, Pennsylvania (1970), and Gary, Indiana (1972), is that they brought together a diverse set of activists, intellectuals, and community organizers from around the country.

Nathan Wright, the executive director of the Department of Urban Work at the Episcopal Diocese of Newark and author of *Black Power and Urban Unrest*, served as chairman of the July 1967 Black Power Conference in Newark, New Jersey. Close to 200 organizations were represented at the downtown Newark meeting with 1,300 people in attendance. Discussions were focused on the economic, political, and educational empowerment of black America. In general assemblies and plenary sessions, conferees resolved to support the economic development of black urban communities nationwide through the expansion of boycotts of white businesses and the creation of small, black-owned businesses and financial institutions. They also agreed to create a lobbying group and a think tank in the nation's capital to influence policy making. Educationally, participants called for more community input and community control of public schools found in predominantly black areas. The conference elucidated the concept of reform nationalism, according to Robert Allen, a scholar of the Black Power movement and author of *Black Awakening in Capitalist America*.[11]

Ron Karenga and Amiri Baraka were the most vociferous proponents of reform nationalism. Karenga was the founder and member of the US Organization in southern California and would be later credited for founding Kwanzaa, an African American cultural holiday held in the closing days of December. Baraka was a Newark-based poet and activist, and founded the Council of African Peoples. The takeaway was that African Americans constituted a particular and unique ethnic group in the United States and as such should work together to reform and integrate themselves into the American body politic and economy.

The BPP organized the second important Black Power conference of the era with its two-day, Revolutionary People's Constitutional

Convention, which began on September 5, 1970, in Philadelphia, Pennsylvania. There are discrepancies over the official number of people in attendance. But conservative estimates suggest that over 10,000 participants attended, many of whom were residents of the City of Brotherly Love. Workshop reports produced at the meeting show an internationalist approach that sought to reconfigure U.S. foreign policy, challenge exploitative economic systems on the domestic front, and change social and personal relationships between individuals and groups within the nation itself. Workshops included discussions on a variety of topics; some of the workshops were Internationalism and Relations with Liberations Struggles around the World, Self-Determination of Street People, Self-Determination of Women, the Family and the Rights of Children, Control and Use of Military and

Activists gather on the steps of the Lincoln Memorial under a banner for the Revolutionary People's Constitutional Convention during the Black Panther Convention, June 19, 1970. (Library of Congress)

Police, Health[care], Revolutionary Art, and Gay Liberation. While some of the ideas and demands expressed in the reports are naïve and an indication of youthful exuberance, together they are robust and offer an insight into the revolutionary aims and principles of the conference.

Limited space here does not allow for discussion of all the workshops, but several warrant our attention. The session on internationalism called for the liberation of Palestine wherein "Palestinians, Jews, Christians and Moslems are equal."[12] Besides calling for a socialist system free from sexism, racism, and classism, the Self Determination for Women session argued that every woman has the right to determine her sexual orientation and that family planning information, materials, and services, including abortion, should be free and "available upon demand."[13] Representatives of the Gay Liberation Movement declared that "all modes of human sexual self-expression deserve protection of the law and social sanction."[14] Health care was deemed a right that should be provided freely by the state, run by community boards at medical facilities, and include health education, preventative care, and mental health services. The 1970 Revolutionary People's Constitutional Conference moved away from reform nationalism and black nationalist principles of the Newark conference to address what has been called a rainbow coalition of ideas.

The third important conference of the classical Black Power era was the National Black Political Assembly held in Gary, Indiana, in March 1972. Unlike the prior two conferences, the Gary conference had the full support of Gary's mayor Richard G. Hatcher who also addressed the assembly. Touting its motto "Unity without Uniformity," the conference brought together celebrities including the actor Sidney Poitier, the actor and singer Harry Belafonte, soul singer Isaac Hayes, politicians, and over 9,000 representatives from major civil rights groups including the Southern Christian Leadership Conference, black nationalist groups including the Congress of Racial Equality, Jesse Jackson's newly formed and reform-oriented organization People to Save Humanity, the intercommunalist BPP, and separatists groups—the Nation of Islam and the Republic of New Afrika, as well as a motley crew of grassroots activists and unaffiliated Black Power adherents.[15] Amiri Baraka, one of three co-conveners (the other two were U.S. congressman Charles Diggs of Michigan and

Richard Hatcher, the mayor of Gary, Indiana), recalls in his autobiography that the assembly was patterned after the U.S. House of Representatives, including proportional representation from states.

The conference did not produce the progressive platforms and resolutions on par with the 1970 Philadelphia Revolutionary People's Constitution Convention. But two resolutions echoed the Philadelphia conference in sentiment if not in specifics. The first called for an end to busing school-age children as a form for education equalization. Rather than transport children out of their community, the first resolution stated, schools in communities of color should be provided adequate funding to educate their children in ways similar schools located in predominantly white neighborhoods and suburbs do. The second resolution presented an international sentiment as it called for peace in Israel and offered support for the Palestinian cause. The assembly also produced what has become known as the Gary Declaration.

The Gary Declaration was essentially a call to arms for the participants at the conference. It criticized the contemporary economic and political environment that created a crisis for segments of the African American population. The crisis of poor educational and housing opportunities and high unemployment and underemployment, they argued, was the result of economic policies that bolstered corporate power and prioritized profit motives over citizens' well-being. In no uncertain terms, it denounced the status quo in politics and race relations. The assembly exclaimed that "the American system does not work for the masses of our people, and it cannot be made to work without radical fundamental change."[16] Accordingly, one of the major shortcomings of the civil rights movement was that its activists and ideologues attempted to integrate into a flawed system. Since the country was marked by "social degradation," black people had no recourse but to be the vanguard of a movement "that places community before individualism, love before sexual exploitation, a living environment before profits, peace before war, justice before unjust 'order,' and morality before expediency."[17] Changing society meant creating an independent black agenda and an independent black political party to make that agenda a reality. The absence of specific, concrete ways to create the independent black political party meant that while the declaration created enthusiasm and excitement among its readership, its vision went largely unrealized. This fact, however, does not detract from its significance or the significance of the two other Black Power meetings in 1967 or 1970. In all three meetings, concerned residents came together, voiced their grievances, spoke truth to power, and continued a tradition of black political protest that began in the early 1930s.

Black Power activism, like the civil rights activism, was decentralized and responded to the political circumstances on the ground in any given location. However, unlike civil rights activists who sought the protection of the federal government, Black Power organizations like the BPP and other organizations were the victims of the FBI's COINTELPRO, a broad surveillance initiative aimed at criminalizing Black Power activists. Such repression did not deter the young and the old in urban areas in the Midwest, northeast, and west as well as thousands in border states from imagining what life would be like without racism and injustice. Legal obstacles had been removed because of civil rights movement victories, but economic and educational opportunities remained out of reach. Undeterred, a coterie of activists emerged during the classical period of Black Power to fill the political void that civil rights activism left empty.

Notes

1. Stokely Carmichael with Ekwueme Michael Thelwell, *Ready for Revolution: The Life and Struggles of Stokely Carmichael [Kwame Ture]* (New York: Scribner, 2003).
2. Peniel Joseph, "Revolution in Babylon: Stokely Carmichael and America in the 1960s," in Manning Marable and Elizabeth Kai Kinton, eds., *The New Black History: Revisiting the Second Reconstruction* (New York: Palgrave Macmillan, 2011), 169–193.
3. Clarence Lang, "Black Power on the Ground: Continuity and Rupture in St. Louis," in Peniel Joseph, *Neighborhood Rebels: Black Power at the Local Level* (New York: Palgrave Macmillan, 2010), 75.
4. Manning Marable, *Malcolm X: A Life of Reinvention* (New York: Penguin Group, 2011), 270.
5. Malcolm X and Alex Haley, *The Autobiography of Malcolm X: As Told to Alex Haley* (New York: Ballantine Books, 1987).
6. Eldridge Cleaver, *Soul on Ice* (New York: Dell Publishing, 1992).
7. Judson Jeffries, *Huey P. Newton: The Radical Theorist* (Jackson: University Press of Mississippi, 2002), 74.

8. Malcolm X and Haley, *The Autobiography of Malcolm X.*
9. Bryan Shih and Yohuru Williams, *The Black Panthers: Portraits from an Unfinished Revolution* (New York: Nation Books, 2016), 163.
10. Rhonda Williams, "The Pursuit of Audacious Power: Rebel Reformers and Neighborhood Politics in Baltimore, 1966–1968," in Peniel Joseph, *Neighborhood Rebels: Black Power at the Local Level* (New York: Palgrave Macmillan, 2010), 216.
11. Robert Allen, *Black Awakening in Capitalist America* (Trenton: Africa World Press, 1992).
12. Kathleen Cleaver and George Katsiaficas, eds., *Liberation, Imagination, and the Black Panther Party* (New York: Routledge, 2001), 289.
13. Ibid., 292.
14. Ibid., 294.
15. Peniel Joseph, *Waiting 'til the Midnight Hour: A Narrative History of Black Power in America* (New York: Henry Holt and Company, 2006).
16. William Van Deburg, *Modern Black Nationalism: From Marcus Garvey to Louis Farrakhan* (New York: New York University Press, 1997), 140.
17. Ibid., 142.

CHAPTER TWO

The Black Panthers in the American South

Despite federal programs, federal and state legislation, U.S. Supreme Court decisions, and the nonviolent direct actions of the modern civil rights movement, many cities and towns throughout the American South continued to be bastions of racism and segregation in the late 1960s and early 1970s. By the time the Black Panther Party (BPP) organized in 1966, the economic, social, and political realities for millions of African Americans in southern states had not changed for decades. There is no doubt that civil rights activists desegregated southern cities and towns and African Americans did not have to contend with de jure segregation. However, African Americans continued to struggle against poverty and structural racism in southern cities and towns when the civil rights movement ended and the Black Panthers were part of many local struggles to end poverty, eliminate structural racism, and halt police brutality in the late 1960s and early 1970.

In Winston-Salem, North Carolina, a dedicated group of activists formed a unit of the National Committee to Combat Fascism (NCCF), an affiliate of the party, in November 1969. NCCF chapters were created that year after the Central Committee conducted nationwide purges to weed out suspected informants. Although not officially recognized as BPP chapters, divisions of the NCCF were understood to be political organizing stations and expected to follow the Ten Point Program and answer to national headquarters. In 1970, the Winston-Salem NCCF became a legitimate chapter of the organization, and despite constant harassment by local police and the FBI, it conducted a free breakfast program for children and operated the Joseph Waddell People's Free Ambulance Service. Nelson Malloy, one of the founders of the Winston-Salem chapter and one of the primary organizers of the free ambulance service, remembers that: "We transported a whole lot of white people with our services too. We would never have been able to get a certificate to operate if we discriminated. The service was for anybody and everybody who needed it."[1] Panthers in Winston-Salem also provided 1,000 bags of food at the Joseph Waddell Free Food Program in July 1972. Hazel Mack, a rank-and-file member in Winston-Salem, remembered that the Black Panthers "would periodically give away bags of groceries in different parts of [Winston-Salem]. My personal favorite was giving away 1,000 bags of groceries with a chicken in every bag."[2] They also conducted a sensational, though unsuccessful, election campaign for city alderman wherein a local Panther, Larry Little, was defeated by less than 100 votes. In Houston, Texas, and New Orleans, Louisiana, the local BPP affiliates were formidable forces with regard to the community empowerment and local and federal law enforcement. What follows is a discussion of the Panthers' activities in those two cities.

Black Panthers in the Space City: Houston, Texas

Houston had a sizable African American population in the late 1960s and early 1970s. Close to 27 percent of the city's inhabitants were African American by 1970. Most lived in three areas of the city, Wards Three, Four, and Five, with poor public infrastructure, segregated and comparatively inferior schools, and police abuse of African Americans. They challenged racism in the city throughout the early 20th century, especially through the National Association for the Advancement of Colored People, but many of their attempts at improving basic quality-of-life issues had been beaten back, leaving the communities' political leadership in the hands of relatively conservative black ministers. In the mid- to late 1960s, however, new political organizations were formed, like the Organization of Black Student Unity (OBSU) and African Americans for Liberation. These groups were comprised primarily of young people and students tired of the slow pace of change in the Houston. Into these changing political times, the Black Panthers inserted themselves.

During a trip to Oakland, California, in the spring of 1968, William Rudd obtained permission to create a Panthers affiliate in Houston. Rudd was in his late twenties, worked as a truck driver, was a native of Houston, and knew the problems facing the African American community there. When Rudd returned to Houston, he recruited approximately 20 young people, including several young women. Most of the recruits were members of OBSU. They optimistically set up their headquarters in the heart of Ward Three with the assistance of a local white intellectual and activists. But before the group could gain momentum, mistrust and fear of FBI (Federal Bureau of Investigation) infiltration compromised the group's ability to create long-lasting, effective programs. Younger members accused Rudd of being an FBI informant and were generally unhappy with the internal politics of the organization. Several of these younger members left within weeks of joining. Besides opening a liberation school and conducting a few political education classes, the Panthers had done little in Houston for several months. Most importantly, they had not succeeded in establishing a free breakfast program, a hallmark of Panther chapters situated elsewhere throughout the nation. Bobby Seale closed the chapter during a speaking engagement in the Houston in November 1968. Initial attempts at forming a BPP affiliate in Houston were abject failures.

The party's revolutionary stance was a hard one to shake in Houston and despite the initial failure at sustaining a Panther presence in the city, young African American activists in Houston continued to be swayed by the organization's revolutionary stance. Carl Hampton, a Houston native and musician, visited Panther headquarters during a tour of California with his soul band. He attended political education classes in the San Francisco Bay Area and worked in various capacities with the headquarters. Political education classes often included a discussion of a variety of books that were listed on the Black Panther Book List (see Table 2.1). Hampton learned the means and ends of the revolution from Seale, Newton, and Cleaver. After returning to Houston, during the winter of 1970, Carl Hampton founded the People's Party II (PP II). The PP II was not officially recognized by the national headquarters of the BPP, but it was also not denied or reviled by it either. Nationally the party was recovering from unintended membership increases and state and federal infiltration, as well as state and federal repression, so to open another branch in the city, after one had already been closed less than two years before, was a political ploy no one wanted to take.

Table 2.1. Black Panther Book List

Malcolm X	*The Autobiography of Malcolm X*
Fanon, Frantz	*Wretched of the Earth*
Nkrumah, Kwame	*I Speak of Freedom*
Davidson, Basil	*The Lost Cities of Africa*
Aptheker, Herbert	*The Nat Turner Slave Revolt*
Aptheker, Herbert	*American Negro Slave Revolts*
Bennett, Lerone	*Before the Mayflower*
Bontemps, Arna W.	*American Negro Poetry—Story of the Negro*
Cronin, E. D.	*Black Moses (The Story of Garvey and the UNIA)*
Du Bois, W.E.B.	*Black Reconstruction in America; Souls of Black Folk; The World and Africa*
Davidson, Basil	*Black Mother, the Years of the African Slave Trade*
Fanon, Frantz	*Studies in a Dying Colonialism*
Franklin, John Hope	*From Slavery to Freedom—Negro in the United States*
Frazier, C. F.	*Black Bourgeoisie*
Harrington, Michael	*The Other America*
Garvey, Marcus	*Garvey & Garveyism—The Philosophy and Opinions of Garveyism*
Herskovitz, Melville J.	*The Myth of the Negro Past*
James, C.L.R.	*A History of Negro Revolts*
Janheinz, John	*MUNTU: The New African Culture*
Jones, Leroi	*Blues People*
Lincoln, C. E	*Black Muslims in America*
Malcolm X	*Malcolm X Speaks*
Memmi, Albert	*The Colonizer and the Colonized*
Nkrumah, Kwame	*Ghana*
Patterson, William L.	*We Charge Genocide*
Rogers, J. A.	*Africa's Gift to America; World's Great Men of Color; 3,000 B.C to 1946 A.D.*
Wesley, Charles H. and Woodson, Carter G.	*The Negro in Our History*
Woodward, C. Van	*The Strange Career of Jim Crow*
Wright, Richard	*Native Son*

Source: http://www.itsabouttimebpp.com/home/sitemap_index.html

The PP II was electrifying. It borrowed heavily from the BPP: it adopted Serve the People Programs and sold the party's newspapers. It also espoused and utilized the party's attempts at building coalitions with progressive white political organizations and forward-thinking political organizations comprised of other people of color. In fact, in Houston, the John Brown Revolutionary League, an organization of white activists, and the Mexican American Youth Organization were staunch allies to PP II.

The PP II also embraced the Panthers' call for armed self-defense and political revolution. Many carried weapons in their cars and on their person always. Carrying a gun was a constitutionally right and was common throughout the Lone Star State. But the pairing of guns with calls for fundamental societal change and an end to police brutality was not a concoction that sat easily with the Houston Police Department and the FBI. PP II was under constant surveillance and shortly after opening its headquarters on Dowling Street, a busy thoroughfare in Ward Three, a predominantly African American community, Carl Hampton had a fatal altercation with police.

It began when David Hines, a party member, was selling newspapers on July 17, 1970. Selling newspapers was not an illegal act. Perhaps, the officers wanted to harass Hines for jaywalking. Maybe Hines actually did something illegal. It was clear that officers did not want Hines selling the *Black Panther*. While the interrogation took place, Carl Hampton arrived on the scene. He was carrying a handgun in a shoulder holster in plain sight. He approached the police as they carried out their duties, a hallmark of the early Panther police patrols in Oakland, California. Panthers from the nearby headquarters joined the scene, armed, to support and defend their comrade. At that point, as if there was not enough confusion, an officer pulled his weapon out of his holster and pointed it at Hampton. The armed Hampton did the same. No shots were fired, but after several tense minutes, Hampton and fellow Panthers returned to headquarters while scores of police cruisers and officers arrived on the scene; armed with riot gear, they surrounded PP II headquarters. Amazingly, the police left the scene within the hour because black residents from Ward Three arrived angry and armed. According to one witness, black residents "told the Houston Police Department they weren't going to shoot [at the PP II headquarters] unless they shot through them."[3]

The police may have left that late afternoon, but the stand-off was not over. Hampton had been charged with assault with intent to murder a police officer. The police wanted him to voluntarily surrender, but Hampton refused, and for 10 days, Panthers and their black, white, and Chicano allies created an impenetrable perimeter around the PP II headquarters. Nine days after the initial altercation between Hampton and the Houston Police, on July 26, police snipers perched on rooftops close to the PP II headquarters. When informed of white men on building rooftops nearby, Hampton, as the leader of the group went to do reconnaissance. He was immediately caught in the crosshairs of a .308 rifle and shot two times in his abdomen and transported to a local hospital where he succumbed to his injuries several hours later. In the interim, a gun fight erupted between police and the armed Panthers in their headquarters. Outnumbered and outgunned, the Panthers headquarters was breached and ransacked by the Houston Police.

Outraged at what some saw as police overreach, at best, or murder, at worst, by the Houston Police, people flocked to the PP II headquarters in support. Community members wanted to lend their help and assist the PP II in whatever way they could. However, the police raid and their siege took its toll on the organization and the PP II was compromised.

PP II members were tied up in legal and state prosecutorial maneuvers, roughed up by police harassment, and arrested for petty violations. James Aaron, a member who was present during the shoot-out on July 26, 1970, was sentenced to a two-year prison term. Others associated with PP II faced a range of charges including assault because of their participation in the shoot-out. On June 8, 1971, police raided PP II headquarters again ostensibly in search of weapons. In early February 1971, PP II members Charles Freeman, Claude Frost, and Kenneth Butler were arrested and charged with violating an obscure statute that prohibited fixing a privately owned automobile on a public street. Too much time, effort, and limited resources were spent in vain attempts to free jailed comrades and too little time was spent serving the people.

Under Willie Rudd's leadership, the first officially sanctioned chapter in Houston managed to sponsor a liberation school and hold political education classes. After Carl Hampton's death at the hands of Houston Police, James Aaron assumed leadership of the PP II, the unsanctioned and unofficially supported affiliate of the party. But since PP II members were mired in legal battles, under his leadership the PP II could only create and manage a pest control program. The People's Free Pest Control Program, as it was called, provided "the community free household extermination of rats, roaches, and other disease-carrying pests and rodents."[4] The program was vital to elderly black Houstonians whose houses were often infested with all sorts of pests.

In late summer 1971, some believed that the BPP and its influence had disappeared from Houston. However, in early autumn 1971, PP II members John Crear, Charles Freeman, and Johnny Coward drove to Oakland with the hope of obtaining permission to restart a chapter in Houston. After meeting Huey P. Newton and receiving official sanction, the three returned to Houston energized and ready to affect change in the Space City. The third and last iteration of the BPP in Houston was by far the most productive.

In 1971 during its third iteration, the BPP of Houston did away with its brief gun-toting past and embraced survival programs. The switch from revolutionary, gun-based rhetoric had happened in chapters and affiliates throughout the nation, and to a certain extent Houston's Panthers were late to the game, but their subsequent efforts were extraordinary. The new and improved Houston chapter organized and sustained a free breakfast program.

Despite the 1960s and early 1970s being prosperous years in the United States, that prosperity did not trickle down to many in African American communities. Lingering effect of Jim Crow made it such that millions of black people did not reap the profits of American prosperity. In Houston and other cities, the Panthers observed and experienced black poverty and responded to it by giving about 50 children food before their school day. Initially, breakfast was served at the Dew Drop Inn, a local bar, because no church or other community organization offered use of its property. Later, Reverend Samuel L. Smith, the minister at Mount Horeb Baptist Church, offered his church to the Panthers, who quickly accepted. The free breakfast program, like others nationwide, was locally based, obtained food from local grocers and sponsors, and followed guidelines from the national office. Headquarters offered a sample menu:

Monday: scrambled eggs, grits, bacon, toast and jelly, juice or milk
Tuesday: hot cakes, sausage, fresh fruit, hot chocolate
Wednesday: eggs, home fries, ham, toast and jam, milk or juice
Thursday: French toast, bacon, fresh fruit, hot chocolate
Friday: Eggs, grits, bacon, toast and jam, milk or juice[5]

Houston Panthers also sponsored a free food program. Headquarters made it clear for the food giveaways when it said that: "the intent of the Free Food Program is to supplement the groceries of Black and poor people until economic conditions allow them to purchase food at reasonable prices."[6] Houstonians were given fresh meat and produce donated and supported by local businesses. At a rally in March 1973, the group gave away close to 500 bags of free food to hungry residents.

The third successful program created and sustained by the Panthers was a free medical screening program. Together with student volunteers from Texas Southern University, Panthers and community members provided free screenings for sickle cell anemia. In 1971, such screenings were part of the party's nationwide Sickle Cell Anemia Research Foundation, which sought to provide screenings for the disease, distribute educational pamphlets and materials, and refer or grant access to necessary assistance by trained medical personnel. The Houston chapter also provided screening for and information about diabetes and hypertension maladies known to go untreated in many black families and communities nationwide. Houston Panthers did not have a medical clinic like other chapters, so screenings took place in busy public spaces like shopping centers.

The second recognized chapter of the BPP in Houston was the most successful of the three BPP affiliates in the city. It gained credibility and support from black residents for three survival programs it sustained and demonstrated the effect that a few dedicated members could have on a community. After six years and three separate affiliates, the BPP of Houston closed its doors in August 1974 when the national staff in Oakland, California, ordered its members to relocate to that city to assist in Bobby Seale's campaign for mayor of Oakland. Some Houstonian Panthers left the Lone Star State for the San Francisco Bay Area, but others refused to leave their home and community. But irrespective of whether they migrated to California like so many African Americans had done before or stayed behind, the members of the BPP of Houston left a legacy of grassroots activism that fought against racism and economic oppression.

Black Panthers in the Crescent City: New Orleans, Louisiana

The BPP gained its footing in New Orleans when a chapter of the NCCF was established in 1970. Brian Hunter was just a young teenager when the Panthers arrived in New Orleans. Decades after their work in the city he remembered: "I was happy that the Panthers had come to New Orleans. They were much needed. They gave the neighborhood and the community a strong sense of pride."[7] The Central Committee at the BPP headquarters, after the insistent request of Geronimo ji Jaga, nee Elmer Pratt, sent Steve Green, Harold Holmes, and George Lloyd to New Orleans to help organize the city's NCCF. There they found a city that boasted a new mayor, Maurice Landrieu, who, though white, was well liked and respected by the city's black residents. Landrieu was known to be forward thinking and was the first mayor in the city's history to appoint African Americans to key city-wide positions. The Crescent City also had Clarence Giarrusso, Landrieu's appointed police chief. Giarrusso was a veteran police officer who was known to keep a cool head and control in tense situations. New Orleans had a substantial black middle class, a cosmopolitan past, a history of interracial political activity, and cultural and social influences from the Caribbean Islands and Latin America. Despite all of these apparent advantages, thousands of the city's black population lived in poverty in public housing projects in the New Orleans's Ninth Ward.

When Green and his comrades arrived in New Orleans, the Ninth Ward is where they started their recruiting. The local control center was set up several city blocks away from Desire, a sprawling public housing project, on Piety Street. With over 1,300 apartments ranging from three to four bedrooms each, by 1970, Desire housed close to 11,000 people, mostly African American. A majority of those housed in that confined and isolated ghetto were younger than 20 years of age. Vermin outnumbered the residents as was clear with large numbers of rats that ran the streets and the roaches that infested what seems to have been every nook and cranny of every apartment. Drug dealers roamed the street pushing drugs to junkies hustled and stole to feed their habits. City emergency services and recreational services were scarce. Public education was inadequate, and even if one managed to obtain quality education, there were no jobs to be had.

Donald Guyton, a 22-year-old Vietnam War veteran, and his wife Barbara were two of the earliest members. Like other chapters of the NCCF and BPP affiliates, the first recruits were young adults, people in the late teenage years and early twenties who had grown up on the streets of New Orleans and wanted to change the political apparatus that kept black people poor in the first place. With so many structural problems facing Desire, the young revolutionaries had a lot to do. With the assistance of Reverend Joseph Putnam, the Panthers helped organize a free breakfast program at St. Francis de Sales Catholic Church. At its height, the program fed close to 125 children per day. Because the Panthers knew that parents' inability to feed their children was not solely an African American problem, but also a problem that poor whites faced, they welcomed children of all races to participate.

When they were not feeding poor children, Crescent City Panthers patrolled the Desire public housing projects in hopes of preventing crime. Drug dealers were put on notice to stop dealing drugs in the community, and if Panthers saw them dealing on the streets or inside housing project hallways, they used force or the threat of force to remove them. Panthers also provided escorts to senior citizens in the housing project to prevent them from being robbed by muggers as they completed their daily errands. In addition, their political education classes taught the young and the old political philosophy and history. For Desire residents, their presence was beneficial, but to local law enforcement, the Panthers were a menace that had to be dealt with and eliminated.

Before Clarence Giarrusso assumed his post as police chief, his brother, Joseph, held the position. Throughout the early summer of 1970, Police Chief Joseph Giarrusso hounded Mayor Landrieu, informing him of the danger that the Panthers posed. He provided FBI surveillance information about the group, monitored the Panthers' movements and recruiting, and hired paid informants to infiltrate the group. In addition, the New Orleans's Police Department Intelligence Unit and the FBI had between three and eight undercover agents infiltrate the group at any time and had the Panthers' headquarters wiretapped. When Clarence Giarrusso became chief of police, he continued the intelligence operation. These covert police actions became the primary cause of the shoot-out at the Piety Street headquarters on September 14, 1970.

Two undercover New Orleans's Police Department agents, Israel Fields and Melvin Howard, managed to covertly join the party in 1970. However, their identities were compromised allegedly when school-age children saw Fields and Howard enter the police department under suspicious pretenses in late August and early September 1970 and informed the Panthers of their real identities in law enforcement. The Panthers did not act on the newfound information immediately; instead, they decided to wait until an acceptable moment arrived to out the covert operatives. In mid-September, it became clear that the police were going to raid the Panther headquarters on whatever legal basis they conjured up. Early in the morning on September 14, Guyton and Charles Scott, a local Panther leader, openly accused Fields and Howard of being police officers, but neither confessed. Rather than beat them, as was done often in other Panther affiliates throughout the country, Guyton and Scott released Fields and Howard. Out on the street and through a growing crowd of Desire residents, Fields and Howard fled and called for backup. Reinforcements came in the form of what some called "a convoy of police buses."[8] When they arrived, they opened fire on the Panthers' building. Officers with high-powered weapons and armored cars exchanged fire with the Panthers who had reinforced their office with sandbags and a cache of shotguns and revolvers.

The siege lasted for about 30 minutes and ended with the Panthers' surrender and their office riddled with bullet holes, but, amazingly, no officer or Panther was hurt. In all, 13 people were arrested after the shoot-out and charged with multiple accounts of attempted murder; the youngest was just 14 years old who just happened to be in the building when the siege took place and was not a member of the party. After close to a year in prison, the Panthers' trial was held on August 7, 1971. The expert defense team was led by attorney Robert Glass who successfully convinced the 12-person jury that the Panthers acted in self-defense when the police attacked.

While their comrades awaited trial, however, those Panthers who were not involved in the September 15, 1970, shoot-out tried to pick up the pieces and continue serving the people. With their headquarters in shambles, they took up residence in a vacant unit in the Desire housing project, apartment 3315, in late October 1970. As with their headquarters on Piety Street, they fortified the apartment with sandbags, firearms, and artillery, ready to defend themselves in the event of another unwarranted police attack. When the housing authority found out that the Panthers were in Desire, they sought to evict them, but the Panthers refused to move. The housing authority may have had the support of the mayor and the police, but the Panthers had the support of the people who lived in Desire and they wanted the Panthers to stay and were ready to fight alongside the group, if necessary. After a month of a heightened police presence in Desire and heightened tensions throughout the Ninth Ward, the police chief and the mayor attempted to negotiate with the Panthers through local clergymen: Jerome LeDoux, William Landon, William Barnwell, Harold Cohen, and Joe Putnam. Using men of the cloth to negotiate with the Panthers on behalf of city officials was a good idea. The Panthers respected the work that the clergy had done for the black poor of New Orleans. In fact, the Panthers had worked with churches to feed children, conduct political education classes, and distribute food in New Orleans and throughout the nation.

But even God's helpers were not going to convince the Panthers to move from the apartment. On November 19, 1970, peaceful negotiations ended and it was decided that force was necessary. New Orleans police officers entered Desire with the intent of evicting the Panthers. It was as if a military standoff was about to take place: armor-plated tanks moved in; police assault rifles were locked and loaded; and police snipers hid in the shadows. A tense standoff began with Panthers located in apartment 3315, the police surrounding and inside the building, and scores, if not hundreds, of BPP sympathizers standing between the two. According to one eyewitness: "the New Orleans Police Superintendent called off an armed four-hour confrontation with a Black Panther group today to prevent what he saw as an impending 'blood bath.'"[9] Marion Brown, a Black Panther in the city, remembers that "when the police tried to evict then, the entire community turned out and stood between the police and the Panthers' office."[10]

At that moment, it appeared that the Panthers had won. By serving the people through their community survival programs, the community helped them survive. An armed incursion was taken off the table, but New Orleans police did not give up their efforts to evict the Panthers. Negotiations had failed. On November 26, Thanksgiving Day, in the early morning hours, there was a knock on the door of apartment 3315. It appeared to be a priest offering materials in support of the Panthers' breakfast program, however, it was a police officer wearing a priest's frock. When the Panthers opened the door, police ran in with weapons drawn, shot one Panther, and took all into custody for trespassing on public property. The police impersonated some of the only people the Panthers trusted to undermine them.

The New Orleans NCCF continued several survival programs, albeit on a smaller scale, after many of its members were released from prison in August 1971. Some members moved to Oakland, California, per the orders of the national leader and found a new political life. Still others, entangled in the cultural mores and life of the Big Easy, stayed behind. The NCCF closed its doors by 1972, but its legacy and desire to help those in need cut a path through the Ninth Ward and New Orleans.

Notes

1. Bryan Shih and Yohuru Williams, *The Black Panthers: Portraits from an Unfinished Revolution* (New York: Nation Books, 2016), 148.
2. Ibid., 157.
3. Charles E. Jones, "Arm Yourself or Harm Yourself: People's Party II and the Black Panther Party in Houston, Texas," in Judson Jeffries, ed., *On the Ground: The Black Panther Party in Communities across America* (Jackson: University of Mississippi Press, 2010), 3–40.
4. David Hilliard, ed., *The Black Panther Party: Service to the People Programs* (Albuquerque: University of New Mexico Press, 2008), 71.
5. Ibid.
6. Ibid., 35.
7. Shih and Williams, *The Black Panthers*, 213.
8. Orissa Arend and Judson L. Jeffries, "The Big Easy Was Anything but for the Panthers," in Judson Jeffries, ed., *On the Ground: The Black Panther Party in Communities across America* (Jackson: University of Mississippi Press, 2010), 224–272.
9. Ibid., 257.
10. Shih and Williams, *The Black Panthers*, 200.

Black Panthers on
the Atlantic
Shore: From
Hope to Death
and Back Again

The Black Panther Party (BPP) had branches all along the northeast coast of the nation. There were chapters in Boston and New Bedford, Massachusetts; Philadelphia, Pennsylvania; and New Haven, Connecticut. All were committed to political and economic change in their city and state and all suffered at the hands of local law enforcement and the Federal Bureau of Investigation (FBI).

When the BPP established a Black Community Information Center in Philadelphia, in 1969, its "objectives," according to historians Omari L. Dyson, Kevin L. Brooks, and Judson L. Jeffries, "were straightforward: to focus on programs and activities that could improve the general welfare of the community."[1] In its attempts to advance social welfare programs and improve the quality of life for thousands of poor blacks in Philadelphia, the BPP organized People's Free Library, a free breakfast program for children, and a free clothing drive. The breakfast program began in North Philadelphia, but was so popular that the group expanded it to three other Philadelphia neighborhoods. Philadelphia Panthers also created the Mark Clark People's Free Medical Clinic where they offered health screenings, preventative medical care, and medical referrals to patients with the assistance of volunteer medical staff.

View of the front stoop, occupied by several women, of the Black Panther Party's Washington chapter community information center Washington DC, circa 1970. The banner hung over the window reads "Free Clothing; Free Bobby; Free Huey," the names referring to incarcerated Panther members Bobby Seale and Huey Newton. (David Fenton/Getty Images)

Like other Panthers throughout the nation, Philadelphia Panthers were highly critical of local political authority. Their public condemnation of institutional racism and police violence against African Americans did not put them in the good graces of the local police. Members were arrested on questionable charges and BPP offices were raided. In a series of police raids on August 31, 1970, Philadelphia police officers armed with riot gear and high-caliber weapons entered three offices and arrested everyone present. One member remembers that, "Each cop took an individual Panther and placed their pistol up the back of our neck and told us to walk down the street backward ... They had the gun, they'd just snatch your pants down and they took pictures of us like that. Then they put us in a wagon and took us to the police station."[2]

Arguably, no chapter suffered more than the New Haven branch wherein Bobby Seale, the national chairman of the organization, and a host of other local leaders were jailed, tried, and eventually released for the death of Alex Rackley. In the early 1970s, the prosecution and subsequent defense of the BPP in New Haven, Connecticut, kept the organization in the newspaper spotlight for years.

Black Panthers in the Bay State: New Bedford and Boston, Massachusetts

During the spring of 1969, several young people including Audrea Jones, Gene Jones, Floyd Hardwick, and Doug Miranda, the area captain, took over the leadership of the Boston chapter of the BPP. The young Marxist-Leninists sought to change black politics in the city and its environs by implementing the BPP's Ten Point Program. They set up their headquarters in Roxbury, Boston's black neighborhood.

Audrea Jones became the principled and strong-willed leader of the group and helped implement several important survival programs. The free clothing program in the Roxbury Mission Hill Housing Project provided children and adults in one of Boston's poorest public housing projects with free clothing. The young Boston Panthers also established a free breakfast program at the Tremont Methodist Church. During the early 1970s, the church was surrounded by one of Boston's black communities, the South End, and had been a liberal institutional supporter of black progressive causes. In fact, in 1964 civil rights activists used the church to establish a freedom school to support black educational endeavors and to challenge and demonstrate against poorly funded black schools. The church was a natural fit for the free breakfast for children program which was reported to have fed nearly 50 children every morning at its height.

Perhaps the most important was the Franklin Lynch People's Free Medical Clinic, which opened in 1970. The clinic was in a trailer parked on a city street and as such wedded the Boston Panthers' radical politics with the radical health politics of the early 1970s to "provide inexpensive alternatives to mainstream medicine . . . to fulfill the health-care needs of underserved groups."[3] Dr. Mary Bassett volunteered with the Panthers' clinic as a college student. She writes that "I recruited Boston-area premed students to perform the screening test. Panther members leafleted public housing buildings the night before, and each Saturday a group of a dozen doctors-to-be fanned out, wearing white jackets, to offer testing in people's homes. Area hospitals provided follow-up for those who screened positive. The sickle cell screening program was a lesson in community health that has never left me. It was more than just a service—it was an organizing tool."[4]

Boston's Panthers were also known to protest, demonstrate, and organize public speaking engagements for the party's leaders. On May 1, 1969, as was the case with other branches and affiliates, they held a Free Huey Newton demonstration. Dozens of Panthers and their supporters assembled at Post Office Square in Boston's Financial District, demanding that their beloved leader, Huey P. Newton, be set free. On November 18, 1970, following his release from prison, flanked by David Hilliard, Elbert "Big Man" Howard, and other Panthers, Huey P. Newton spoke to hundreds of students, activists, and intellectuals at the Rogers Center at Boston University. That year they also organized a march that comprised white students and black activists down Tremont Street. When the New Haven chapter imploded after Alex Rackley's murder, many from the Boston chapter relocated to New Haven to rebuild that chapter.

According to historian Jama Lazerow, "Boston exercised authority over New Bedford, determining its leadership, moving people in and out, even controlling its finances."[5] As early as January 1970, the Black Panthers were organizing young people in New Bedford, Massachusetts. In July of that year, with the permission of Boston Panthers, a branch of the National Committee to Combat Fascism was established by local activists. There, local Panthers, many of Cape Verdean descent, like Johnny Viera, Frank "Parky" Grace, and Dukie Matthews set up a free clothing program, a breakfast program, a liberation school, and political education classes. The group even organized sickle cell anemia testing throughout the Whaling City's schools. On July 31, 1970, after weeks of unrest in New Bedford, local police raided the National Committee to Combat Fascism (NCCF) headquarters. Unlike altercations between law enforcement and Panthers in other cities, the armed New Bedford Panthers, though desiring an armed revolution, relented. Ten members were indicted by a grand jury, but only one member served jail time. In early 1972, by order of the Boston chapter, the New Bedford NCCF closed its doors.

The Black Panther Party in New Haven, Connecticut

The New Haven chapter of the BPP was organized in the winter and spring of 1969 by José René Gonzalvez and Ericka Huggins when national headquarters was in the process of purging membership rolls throughout the nation. Gonzalvez is reported to have been a native of Cuba, fluent in Spanish, and moved to the United States with his parents as an adolescent. In Bridgeport, Connecticut, Gonzalvez used his bilingual skills to reach out to the growing Puerto Rican population there. Gonzalvez told William Perez of the *Hartford Courant* that he and his associates were "the only ones to have been authorized by national headquarters" to work "underground" to "help the people help themselves."[6]

Ericka Huggins was born into a black working-class family and raised in Washington, D.C. She attended Lincoln University, a historically black institution in Pennsylvania where she married John Huggins a Vietnam War veteran. In 1967, the two left Pennsylvania for Los Angeles, California, to be more active participants in the black freedom struggle. Upon enrolling at the University of California, Los Angeles (UCLA), Ericka and John joined the BPP. In southern California, the local chapter of the party was rivaled by the US Organization, a black nationalist cultural organization whose leader, Ron Karenga, wanted to transform the politics of black America through African-inspired culture and practices. During a January 1969 feud over the leadership of UCLA's Black Student Union, John Huggins was killed by members of the US Organization. Devastated but determined, the young widow took her newborn and husband's body and moved to New Haven, Connecticut.

Gonzalvez had only been in the state for several weeks when Edward J. Callum of the Connecticut Citizens Anti-Communist Committee besmirched the nascent organization, calling them "revolutionary peddlers of hate" and a "Black Mafia." Callum's fears were echoed in the memos and files sent between the Special Agent in Charge (SAC) of the FBI's New Haven Office and then director J. Edgar Hoover. Although an official Connecticut chapter was not recognized by national Panthers headquarters until March 1969, J. Edgar Hoover instructed the New Haven's SAC to "initiate a counterintelligence program against the BPP" and "disrupt" its work as early as January of that year.

Slowly, however, the young organizers' work paid off and their approach and energy attracted young people in their teens and early twenties. With Ericka Huggins as the education director and Gonzalvez filling the position of state captain, the two met with a variety of community groups and spoke to anyone interested in the party's message.

In March 1969, the Connecticut BPP set up its headquarters in the Hill District, a predominantly black section of New Haven. It made modest gains in membership throughout the state in March and April 1969 with close to two dozen members. One of the most active new recruits was Warren Kimbro. At age 35, he was more than 10 years older than the other local Panthers and worked as an organizer for Community Progress Inc., a citywide antipoverty program, in the Dwight neighborhood of New Haven. His townhouse on Orchard Street in the Dwight neighborhood became Connecticut headquarters of the Connecticut chapter of the party. Shortly after joining the BPP, he accompanied Gonzalvez and Huggins around town and around the state explaining the party's platform and pointing out injustices meted out to black people in New Haven.

New Haven Panthers joined with local residents of the Hill and Dwight neighborhoods to oppose the construction of Route 34, a Connecticut state highway. In the late 1960s, the state of Connecticut acquired large tracts of land to build the highway to connect New Haven to the outlying suburbs. In the process, hundreds of black families and scores of businesses were slated for displacement to make way for a highway that would permit middle-class whites to commute from the city to the suburbs. The young activists understood the construction project through the lens of racism and capitalism. "If we allow Rt. 34 to be built," they declared, "then we are condoning capitalism and racism. By this we mean America can build roads while people have no homes. America can build garages when people have no food." Community opposition forced the Connecticut Department of Transportation to abandon the project in the early 1970s. The New Haven BPP was one group in a larger opposition, but their participation demonstrated to the budding activists that community partnerships and mobilization could bring desired results.

In spring 1969, Ericka Huggins offered classes in Marxism and BPP ideology and tried to recruit people to help her with a health clinic she was planning to create in New Haven's black community. Along with Panthers and sympathizers throughout the country, Connecticut members organized a solidarity demonstration in New Haven and in front of the Federal Building in Hartford on May 1, 1969, to bring attention to Huey P. Newton's imprisonment at the San Luis Obispo Men's Colony in California. Carrying placards featuring images of Newton and "Free Huey" signs, the demonstration was used to bring attention to racism in the criminal justice system through points 8 and 9 of the organization's platform.

Despite these successes, mistrust and FBI counterintelligence activities began to take their toll on the chapter. The FBI had the chapter under close surveillance and initiated several activities to create tensions between the local party and the black community. Local police departments used "lawful harassment and successful prosecution" to disgrace BPP leadership. The party's phones were wiretapped and the organization was infiltrated by at least one informant who provided weekly, if not daily, reports about the chapter to New Haven's SAC.

To deal with informants, real or imagined, the Central Committee stopped the induction of members partially "[to] get rid of agents and provocateurs." Bobby Seale's and Huey P. Newton's uncertainty of the trustworthiness of the local chapters and memberships filtered down to the grassroots and the Connecticut BPP did not escape this pattern of suspicion. Local members developed an underlying mistrust of the state's leaders.

During a trip to party headquarters in April 1969, Jose Gonzalvez and Lonnie McLucas were embroiled in a conflict. Jewelry and money

The Black Panthers protest at a courthouse in New York City, April 11, 1969. (David Fenton/Archive Photos/Getty Images)

were taken from a Panther's home in Oakland, and Gonzalvez and McLucas accused each other of the crime. Simultaneously, Ericka Huggins and Warren Kimbro were critical of Gonzalvez's work in the party. Kimbro may have resented that the party's national leaders sent Gonzalvez, a Cuban immigrant, to organize black Americans in Connecticut. Perhaps Gonzalvez was more strident in his use of party rhetoric than necessary, and, at times, it bordered on the irresponsible. In one instance, he vowed to kill drug dealers in black communities throughout the state. In another, he threatened elected officials with "pistols, rifles, shotguns, machine guns, and grenades." He went to Charlotte, North Carolina, to organize a chapter there without permission from headquarters in early May 1969 and was reprimanded. He was stripped of his rank as state captain of the Connecticut chapter after Ericka Huggins wrote a letter to national headquarters informing them that among other things Gonzalvez had "misrepresented the party," "rejected the party's discipline," "failed to provide adequate leadership," and did not study politics.[7] Gonzalvez left the party and resurfaced in Greensboro, North Carolina, later that year.

Gonzalvez's expulsion did not end intraparty conflict in New Haven or the FBI's counterintelligence. On May 12, 1969, New Haven's SAC hatched another plan to "make an anonymous telephone call from New Haven to the national BPP headquarters."[8] During the call, the unidentified caller would accuse local party leaders of abusing power and misusing party funds. The hope was that leaders of the national office would investigate such claims and increase friction among local members and between the local chapter and headquarters. Permission to forward with the counterintelligence plan was never granted because such a call was not necessary. The wheels of disruption were already in motion and the New Haven BPP was on the road to self-destruction.

The Murder of Alex Rackley

From the time that New Haven's FBI made its initial request for permission to make an anonymous phone call from New Haven to California headquarters on May 12 and Hoover's review of and response to the request on May 28, not only was Jose Gonzalvez expelled, but also the Connecticut BPP was involved in the murder of Alex Rackley, a young Panther from New York City.

Rackley was 19 years old in early 1969 he when traveled to New York City from Florida and began hanging around the Panther offices where he became a martial arts instructor at the Harlem chapter. On May 17, he joined "Crazy George" Sams and other Panthers on a trip to New Haven to help prepare for Bobby Seale's talk at Yale University and help organize the New Haven chapter. Sams had been a member of the party for a couple of years and had even been Stokely Carmichael's bodyguard during Carmichael's short tenure as the organization's prime minister. He was known to be undisciplined and abusive and carried several guns in his overcoat. The infiltration of informants nationwide, the subsequent fear of informant infiltration along with New Haven members' fear of Sams, and Sams's ability to intimidate the younger New Haven comrades, collectively allowed him to arrive in New Haven and take over the fledgling chapter's offices.

On May 18, Sams declared that Rackley was a police informant and collaborated with New Haven members to bind, torture, and interrogate Rackley. On May 20, Rackley was taken to the banks of the Coginchaug River. Sams gave Kimbro a .45 automatic pistol and told him to shoot Rackley. Kimbro followed orders and shot Rackley in the head. Sams then gave the gun to McLucas. McLucas followed orders and shot Rackley in the chest. His scalded, bloody corpse was found the next day by a fisherman.

On May 21, the New Haven Police along with undercover FBI agents raided Connecticut party headquarters and arrested Warren Kimbro, Ericka Huggins, Jeannie Wilson, Rose Smith, George Edwards, Maude Francis, Francis Carter, and Margaret Hudgins and charged them with murder and conspiracy to commit murder. One week later, Loretta Luckes was arrested and charged with murder, conspiracy to commit murder, kidnapping, conspiracy to commit kidnapping, and binding with criminal intent. Both Landon Williams, a field marshal from party headquarters, and Rory Hithe, a young Panther from Oakland, were present during Rackley's interrogation, and fled to Denver, Colorado, where they were eventually extradited to stand trial. Lonnie McLucas fled to Salt Lake City, Utah, and was also extradited to New Haven. George Sams eluded police in several cities, but was eventually captured in Toronto, Canada, and returned to New Haven in August 1969 where he testified that Bobby Seale gave the order to kill Rackley. State prosecutors believed him and had Seale extradited to Connecticut to stand trial for murder-related charges.

The Panthers' outcry against the New Haven arrests was vociferous. The BPP always maintained that Rackley's murder was orchestrated by forces bent on undermining the Panthers. In its initial response, BPP headquarters suggested that Rackley's murder was a conspiracy cooked up by federal, state, and or local authorities. "It is clear if there was really someone who has been killed," *The Black Panther* published, "then it's got to be the CIA, FBI and local pigs who killed this person, or it's just someone killed that the pigs want to blame on the Black Panther Party as a means to charge the Connecticut Panther leadership with a capital crime."[9] One month later, *The Black Panther* printed that "Rackley was an excellent organizer who was murdered by the pigs." The eight Panthers who were imprisoned "have been framed on trumped-up charges." Cornell Wright, a Panther from Hartford, Connecticut, hypothesized that police framed those arrested in order "to kill a rising political force."[10]

With time, the BPP's official position on Rackley's death tempered, especially after George Sams, Warren Kimbro, and Lonnie McLucas confessed to having killed Alex Rackley. In "The Black Panther Party Position on the Murder of Alex Rackley," the party remained insistent that the state and federal authorities were involved in Rackley's death. However, Sams orchestrated Rackley's torture and gave the order for him to be shot. New Haven Panthers were "young," "immature," and "impressionable" and, therefore, could not "be blamed for what George Sams did or made them do under the threat of death." Headquarters also assumed some of the blame for the incident by allowing "a maniac such as George Sams to come into our party."

With party members in jail or awaiting trial, the New Haven chapter fell apart. Loretta Luckes pleaded guilty to "conspiracy to kidnap resulting in death" in December 1969. George Sams and Warren Kimbro pleaded guilty to second-degree murder. Lonnie McLucas proclaimed his innocence and went to trial. Represented by the progressive attorney Theodore Koskoff, he was convicted of conspiracy to murder and sentenced to a maximum jail time of 15 years in August 1970. He spent several years in prison and was subsequently released in 1973. George Edwards, Rose Marie Smith, and Margaret Hudgins pleaded guilty in September 1970 and received suspended sentences. All three served over a year in prison and were released in October 1970. Francis Carter spent over a year in prison, but he was released on a lesser charge because of insufficient evidence. Landon Williams and Rory Hithe fought hard to prevent extradition to Connecticut, but eventually lost their fight. The two served 20 months in the state penitentiary before pleading guilty to conspiracy to murder. Their sentences were suspended and they left the state in 1971.

Rackley's murder had far-reaching effects. Nationally, FBI and police raided party offices under the pretense of looking for George Sams, Rory Hithe, and Landon Williams. Locally, from late May 1969 to early fall 1969, the New Haven BPP was virtually defunct. Members who were not charged in the Rackley murder left the party, and sympathizers distanced themselves from the organization.

Rebuilding New Haven

Alex Rackley's murder had tarnished the group's image, but the national BPP leadership was not prepared to give up on New Haven, especially with Bobby Seale and Ericka Huggins incarcerated and awaiting trial. To rebuild the party, organizers from East Coast cities were sent to New Haven to repair relationships with the black community, create survival programs for city residents, and rally support for Seale and Huggins. The constant arrival of organizers from other cities in fall 1969 bolstered membership so that there were between 15 and 20 full-time Panthers in New Haven by January 1970.

The transplanted Panthers were experienced and enthusiastic organizers. Robert Webb, from California, gave stability to the group and clarity of focus. Jacob Bethea, a Panther from New York City, told a reporter from the *Hartford Courant* that the primary objective of the new arrivals was to create free breakfast programs, health centers, and liberation schools. Roscoe Lee, an organizer from Harlem, New York, declared that the Panthers "are teaching the people to help themselves to free their minds." Doug Miranda relocated to New Haven from Boston and became the Connecticut state captain. He recalls that New Haven was a "hard nut to crack in terms of organizing." Within nine months through tireless community outreach, however, black people's fears and negative opinions dissipated making the Panthers a viable political player in New Haven's black community once again.

The *People's News Service* and the survival programs the party started were critical to Panther community tactical outreach. The *Service*, which ran from October 1969 to June 1970 and was edited by Charles Pinderhughes, was an 8- to 12-page handout that included articles on local and national news and offered the Panthers the opportunity to inform the community of their perspective and work. With the paper in hand, Panthers combed through black neighborhoods, circulated it, and discussed the party's platform, approach, and programs with anyone who would listen. Because the articles were written in an intriguing fashion and could be easily understood by New Haven's black residents, it offered numerous opportunities to build support for the party. In addition to the *People's News Service*, the New Haven BPP also restarted and expanded the free Breakfast for children program, and initiated other programs including a legal first aid program, political education classes, a free health clinic, a free clothing program, a free library program, and community discussion groups.

The free breakfast for children program was one of the first survival programs the Panthers organized in Oakland, California. The program was set up in New Haven in the early spring 1969, but was quickly dismantled after Rackley's murder. When students began classes in the fall of 1969, however, Panthers were there with hot meals. Joel Brown, a Panther transplant from Boston, was one of the primary organizers of the breakfast program. He and other members successfully lobbied the United Newhallville Organizations to allow the BPP to use the Newhallville Teen Lounge at 179 Shelton Avenue for its John Huggins Memorial Free Breakfast for Children Program. During the 1969 fall term, breakfast was served from 7 a.m. to 8:30 a.m. with food and equipment donated from local merchants. Transportation was provided by the Panthers free of charge to the lounge and then to school for children who required it. Its advertising flier circulated around the community and its *People's News Service* informed community members that the program was a "socialistic [one] designed to help all people not just a 'chosen few.'"

Nationally, the free breakfast for children program had a threefold purpose. The first, and most obvious, purpose was to feed hungry children and support families. Lyndon B. Johnson's Great Society programs, anti-poverty programs, and Model Cities programs did not have the desired effects for poor families of all colors nationwide. Hunger was a problem, especially in black communities, and the Panthers knew it. Many members had experienced it. They knew personally that going to school with an empty stomach made it difficult for students to concentrate on their studies. The second purpose was to elevate poverty and hunger as issues requiring the attention of local communities and national leaders. The third purpose of the breakfast for children program, according to Doug Miranda, was to take Marxist theory and put it into practice, to move beyond academic chatter, and bring "together the mind and the body" to improve the basic quality of life for all Americans, especially black people.

In the spring of 1970, the BPP national headquarters directed chapters throughout the country to create health centers, People's Free Medical Clinics (PFMC), in black communities. Frances Carter,

Carolyn Jones, and Rosemary Mealey were the moving force behind the creation of the John Huggins Free Health and Research Center located at 27 Dixwell Avenue, an abandoned storefront, which opened in January 1971. Gussie Pheanious, the center coordinator in early 1971, maintained that the PFMC was part of the revolutionary spirit of the party. Like the free breakfast program, the clinic offered the New Haven BPP an opportunity to put its theory into revolutionary practice. "People will make the revolution," Pheanious told a reporter, "with the help of a healthy body, adequate housing and full stomach. The mind can't function if the body doesn't function."[11] As with their breakfast program, Panthers received assistance from the communities they served via local merchants and surrounding schools including the University of New Haven whose student government donated $1,000.

The PFMC was modest. It was equipped with a waiting room, clerical space, two examination rooms, and a laboratory and was staffed by physicians from the Medical Committee for Human Rights, several Yale University medical students, a nurse, lab technician, and community members. The Health and Research Center, like other PFMCs throughout the country, provided a range of services. It provided preventative care and first aid, gynecological services, dental referrals, pediatric care for children, and sickle cell anemia testing, as well as diabetes care management and awareness. All services were provided free of charge and the clinic reportedly treated close to 400 patients during the winter of 1971. Most importantly, the center empowered individuals with knowledge to improve their health and make informed health decisions, two critical issues that biomedical facilities in the 1970s failed to provide to black people.

Free Bobby, Free Ericka!

Bobby Seale, who had been in New Haven for a speaking engagement when Rackley was tortured and killed in May 1969, was accused by State Attorney Arnold Markle of ordering Rackley's death and was charged with kidnapping, conspiracy to commit kidnapping, murder in the first degree, and conspiracy to commit murder. Huggins was present during the torture, but did not participate in and did not see Kimbro or McLucas shoot Rackley. She was charged with kidnapping, conspiracy to commit kidnapping, murder in the first degree, conspiracy to commit murder, and binding with intent to commit crime. Their trial began on November 17, 1970, and was, along with the rallies surrounding the trial, one of the most important events in BPP history. It was also among most dramatic events in the history of the BPP in Connecticut.

The Panthers continued to oppose the arrests, detention, and trials of their New Haven members, viewing such actions as attacks on the leftist groups in general and the BPP in particular. Bobby Seale saw himself as a political prisoner being tried "because we are dedicated in this very same revolutionary way of serving the people with these cooperative, socialistic community programs." *The Black Panther* declared that "[the] attempt to murder Chairman Bobby Seale coldbloodedly in the Electric Chair is an open provocation and the ultimate aggression against Black people. It is a calculated step taken by fascist pigs in the unfolding of their vicious blueprint of genocide against Black people." The group agreed with members of the Students for a Democratic Society (SDS) who argued that "charges against the New Haven Panthers, which have been trumped up by the government and police, are intended to intensify race hatred by playing upon the lies and myths instilled in white people by the educational system and the mass media."

In September and early October 1969, Panthers worked with community groups and Yale University students to form the Coalition for Defense of the Black Panthers. The coalition comprised white and black professionals and local political and cultural organizations. In its October press conference, the organization issued a statement detailing that its primary objectives were to inform New Haven residents of the BPP's survival programs and constitutional rights, respond to the negative media reports about the Panthers, and fund-raise to support the Panthers in their legal battles. Each organization provided statements about its participation, and all were all united in their critique of what they saw as a public persecution of the Panthers. They also stated their concerns about the possibility of any Black Panther receiving a fair trial in Connecticut. None of the organizations or individuals argued that the Panthers should not stand trial. They believed in the validity of the criminal justice system. Their sentiments were best articulated by the Dixwell Legal Rights Association whose press statement maintained that "it is essential to demand and work constructively for a legal system which protects the constitutional rights of all defendants, regardless of their political or social beliefs. Furthermore, every citizen and all community groups must bear this responsibility by actively seeking a fair trial for the arrested members of the Black Panther Party."

With Robert Abramovitz, a local physician, as chair of the coalition, members saw their work as educational in nature and involved the following activities: to issue public statements, act as a clearinghouse for accurate and pertinent information about civil liberties, and arrange for informed speakers who used every forum available to discuss the Panthers' situation. Members spoke at parent–teacher association meetings, neighborhood groups, and club meetings. Yale Divinity School students were tasked with speaking at local houses of worship. Myrna Fichtenbaum, a founding member of the coalition, noted that the most important issue for groups and individuals was to remember to stay on message: "try to convince people in the city to speak out about a fair trial."

The Panthers welcomed the coalition's help, but did not depend on it. Panthers were also in the community and on university campuses trying to gain support. On October 22, 1969, Doug Miranda delivered an address at the University of Connecticut to a mostly white audience to "clear a lot of mistaken ideas . . . young college students have about the Black Panther Party."[12] The speech was recorded and transcribed by the FBI. In it, Miranda provided a historical overview of the BPP and noted the ideological contributions of Malcolm X. He proceeded to enumerate and discuss the BPP's Ten Point Program and the Panthers' survival programs, and connect the Panthers' political struggle to anti-colonial and anti-racist programs around the world. One month later in November, the Panthers cosponsored a People's Rally with People to Free the Panthers on the New Haven Green in an attempt to bring more attention to the arrests and trials of their comrades. Twenty-one buses shuttled people to the Green and over 2,000 people participated of whom many were University of Connecticut students who had heard the Panthers' story and were politically energized by Miranda one month before.

Widespread support for the Panther cause was elusive in 1969. Perhaps it was because the New Haven BPP was focused on creating and sustaining survival programs. Maybe it was because blacks and whites had not overcome the shock of a murder of a Black Panther in the Elm City. Nonetheless, the limited support did not discourage the Panthers, and in 1970, a wellspring of support emerged. One of the most important people in this support was Jean Genet, a white French political activist and writer.

Genet had been interested in African American culture and politics for some time and was in his early sixties when he came out in support of the Panther cause. During the 1960s, Genet became increasingly concerned with issues of racial discrimination around the world and saw the Panthers' arrest, detention, and trial as a battle in the class war between the capitalist class and the proletariat. On March 18, 1970, Genet joined David Hilliard, the chief of staff of the BPP, and Doug Miranda at a rally at the Albert N. Jorgenson Auditorium at the University of Connecticut, Storrs.[13] He addressed the crowd in French using an interpreter. "Bobby Seale's trial," he noted, "is a political trial of the Black Panther Party and on a more general basis a race trial held against all of American blacks." In garnering support for the Panthers, he beseeched the predominantly white audience of 2,000 to mobilize around the trial because "your intellect and physical ability, your moral imperatives are capable of making you act faster than I and with greater efficiency." Throughout 1970, he traveled around Connecticut and the country to speak on behalf of the Panthers.

Another support system came from the New Haven Panther Defense Committee (NHPDC) in 1970. The NHPDC originated in the fall of 1969 and was responsible for the November 22, 1969, rally on the New Haven Green. The organization comprised white working-class Marxists from SDS, the American Independent Movement, the Patriot Party, and members of the BPP. They supported the political program of the Panthers and saw their work as not only freeing their imprisoned Black Panther colleagues, but also advancing the work of leftist organizations. One of their most important rallies was a teach-in at Yale Law School Auditorium on September 25, 1970. At the teach-in, the NHPDC stressed the need for whites to join in the struggle to free the Panthers and fight for social, political, and economic justice. Further, the NHPDC articulated the interconnected nature of war, racism, and capitalism in the lives of black Americans. The Vietnam War, they argued, resulted in more black soldiers dying than whites; racism presented a "special oppression" for black people as "an entire people"; and capitalism "breeds racism." Seeing racism from a structural level helped privileged white students see that racism was more than white personal prejudices and moved the discussion of race and racism from the personal to the institutional level.

Ericka Huggins's and Bobby Seale's Trial

Huggins had been imprisoned and refused bail since her arrest in May 1969. Seale was extradited from California in March 1970 and refused bail. Arnold Markle was the prosecuting attorney for the state and Superior Court Judge Harold M. Mulvey presided over the case. Charles Garry and David Rosen, Seale's defense attorneys, and Catherine Roraback, Huggins's defense attorney, tried to get all charges dismissed using legal arguments and several motions. One of the defense's pretrial motions argued that the police did not have probable cause—sufficient reason—to raid the Connecticut Panther headquarters and make arrests on May 22, 1969, shortly after Rackley's body was found.[14] Judge Mulvey ruled that the police had probable cause, and thus, the arrests were warranted given the testimony of two police informants who had infiltrated the Panthers and corroborating statements from Francis Carter who had been arrested and questioned by the police on May 21. In March 1970, Judge Mulvey rejected a motion by the defense, which argued that Seale's, Huggins's, and other Panthers' cases should be dismissed because their Sixth Amendment rights were violated when the state did not allow the accused to confront and question state material witnesses, Maude Francis and Aletta Wilson, two juvenile Panthers who testified against those jailed during bail hearings. Defense attorneys tried again to have the charges dismissed in October 1970 when they argued that pretrial publicity in the state of Connecticut would make it impossible for their clients to receive a fair jury trial. They cited newspaper stories and New Haven Police Department press releases and called as witnesses representatives from newspapers, radio, and television to discuss the extent of their coverage of the Rackley murder. Again, Mulvey was not convinced of their arguments and dismissed the motions. With all legal means exhausted, Seale and Huggins were scheduled to be tried.

Because the 12-member jury was to be comprised of residents in New Haven and its environs, one of the most important strategies available to defense attorneys was to make sure the jury was as fair and impartial as possible. The attorneys had to be sure that jurors were not unduly influenced by the media coverage, police press conferences and statements, or endemic racism. All things being equal, given the black population of New Haven and its suburbs in the early 1970s for blacks to be properly represented on the jury, 3 of the 12 jurors would have had to be African American. For 17 weeks, the prosecution and defense team questioned potential jurors to determine their suitability for jury duty. In all, 1,034 individuals were interviewed to fill the 12-person jury. When jury selection concluded, 12 standing jurors were selected, 5 black and 7 whites, with 2 alternates, 1 black and 1 white. The alternates listened to all evidence but could not take part in deliberations unless one or two of the standing jurors became ill. The trial against Bobby Seale and Ericka Huggins lasted a little over two months, but the prosecution, despite putting George Sams on the stand, was unable to prove its case beyond a shadow of a doubt and the 12-person jury could not reach a unanimous decision. On May 25, 1971, Judge Harold Mulvey declared a mistrial and Seale and Huggins were released from state custody.

Notes

1. Omari L. Dyson, Kevin L. Brooks, and Judson Jeffries, "Brotherly Love Can Kill You: The Philadelphia Branch of the Black Panther Party," in Judson L. Jeffries, ed., *Comrades: A Local History of the Black Panther Party* (Bloomington: Indiana University Press, 2007), 224.
2. Members of the Black Panther Party, stripped, handcuffed, and arrested after Philadelphia police raided the Panther headquarters, August, 1970. http://explorepahistory.com/displayimage.php?imgId=1-2-1710.
3. Alondra Nelson, *Body and Soul: The Black Panther Party and the Fight against Medical Discrimination* (Minneapolis: University of Minnesota Press, 2011), 82.
4. Mary Bassett, "Beyond Berets: The Black Panthers as Health Activists," *American Journal of Public Health* 106, no. 10 (October 2016): 1741–1743. Accessed April 4, 2017. www.ncbi.nlm.nih.gov/pmc/articles/PMC5024403.
5. Jama Lazerow, "The Black Panthers at the Water's Edge: Oakland, Boston, and the New Bedford 'Riots of 1970,'" in Yohuru Williams and Jama Lazerow,

eds., *Liberated Territory: Untold Local Perspectives of the Black Panther Party* (Durham and London: Duke University Press, 2008), 85–135.

6. William Perez, "Black Panthers Organizing in State," *Hartford Courant*, February 9, 1969, 1A.

7. Paul Bass and Douglas W. Rae, *Murder in the Model City: The Black Panthers, Yale, and the Redemption of a Killer* (New York: Basic Books, 2006), 85.

8. Memo, Special Agent in Charge, New Haven to Director, FBI, May 12, 1969, http:/vault.fbi.gov/BlackPantherParty.

9. N.a., "Pig Conspiracy against Conn. Panthers," *The Black Panther*, May 31, 1969, 3.

10. N.a., "Fascist Forces Move Nationwide to Destroy Black Panther Party," *The Black Panther*, June 21, 1969, 5.

11. Edward Woodyard, "The Panthers and Huggins Health Center," *The New Haven Register*, March 26, 1972, 3B; Nelson, *Body and Soul*, 96.

12. Doug Miranda, Speech delivered at the University of Connecticut, October 22, 1969, John R. Williams Papers, Box 3, Folder 17, Manuscripts and Archives, Yale University.

13. Rally at University of Connecticut, Storrs, March 18, 1970, John R. Williams Papers, Box 5, Folder 34, Manuscripts and Archives, Yale University.

14. Charles Hines, "8 Panthers Held in Murder Plot: Body Found in River at Middlefield," May 22, 1969, 1.

CHAPTER FOUR

The Black
Panthers in the
Midwest

The Black Panther Party (BPP) had chapters and affiliates in
midwestern cities that were home to large African American populations that were commonly associated with black political activism and
also in midwestern cities that were home to smaller African American
populations. In cities and large and small, African Americans suffered
from similar problems: unemployment and underemployment, crum-
bling public infrastructure, poor housing conditions, and inadequate
public schools. To be sure, by the late 1960s, African Americans had
resided in midwestern states for generations, but their limited political
power combined with structural racism made them invisible to white
politicians. Throughout the Midwest, black people were forced to
reside in segregated enclaves. Inured by the limited gains from the civil
rights movement in their cities, young African American activists in
Chicago, Illinois; Detroit, Michigan; Milwaukee, Wisconsin; Des
Moines, Iowa; Kansas City, Missouri; and Omaha, Nebraska gravi-
tated to the party's revolutionary stance and survival programs.

Motown Radicals: Black Panthers in Detroit, Michigan

In the late 1960s, Detroit, Michigan, was 40 percent black. Tens of thousands of the African Americans lived in the Twelfth Street District, a poor, congested, and crime-infested neighborhood. It was in the Twelfth Street district that riots erupted during the hot July of 1967. Many black organizations sprouted in the city to disable structural racism, raise class consciousness, negotiate with city officials on behalf of the city's black residents, and address problems of urban living. The Nation of Islam had a mosque in the city, and like Muslim members elsewhere, the branch attempted to sow the seed of self-reliance, modesty, and black conservatism among Detroit's blacks. The Detroit Revolutionary Action Movement, an African American Marxist group, organized black workers in Detroit's ubiquitous automobile industry and orchestrated strikes at the Chrysler car manufacturing plant in the city in May 1968. The Republic of New Africa (RNA) was also active in Detroit. The RNA demanded reparations for African Americans to acknowledge centuries of abuse, slavery, and neglect as well as a portion of the southeastern United States to set up their own sovereign country and government.

When Ron Scott, Eric Bell, Jackie Spicer, George Gilles, and Victor Stewart established the Black Panther branch in Detroit in May 1968, they did not enter a black community that had been immune from black political organizing. Police harassment, violence, and fear of spy infiltration caused the Detroit branch to close in less than a year, but it was reconstituted as a National Committee to Combat Fascism (NCCF) affiliate with Malik McClure as its chairman. Like Panther affiliates in other parts of the nation, Detroit Panthers organized political education classes and survival programs including a free breakfast program, a pest extermination program, free barbering services, and a free health clinic staffed by volunteer doctors. They also offered a new vision of self-defense to a community that largely, up to that point, had been afraid to use armed opposition against a predominantly white Detroit police force that used violence and intimidation against the city's black community.

Under McClure's leadership, the Detroit Panthers created what historian Ahman Rahman calls "underground self-defense cells" for "armed opposition to the police."[1] It is unclear how many cells existed throughout the Motor City or how many Panthers participated. However, fear of police and FBI infiltration kept involvement low and participation secret. Some of these underground Panthers raided city drug dealers, stole marijuana and money to use for the revolution, and destroyed heroin and other hard drugs. Others acquired weapons. Several were so emboldened that they attacked police to retaliate against police brutality or defend themselves during police raids. In summer 1970, Lawrence White, a former marine, along with several other Panthers attacked and wounded two white patrolmen while they sat in their police cruiser. When police tried to apprehend him at his home White refused to surrender. Not knowing that White stockpiled weapons and several gas masks, Detroit police used tear gas to force him out. White kept officers at bay for 10 hours and only surrendered when he ran out of ammunition. At trial, he refused to name his co-conspirators resulting in a 15- to 30-year prison term. One year later, the underground cells were dismantled when its leaders were hunted down one by one by the FBI and its leaders jailed.

Above ground, Panthers in the Motor City continued to serve the people, but like their underground comrades, their activism suffered setbacks. On October 24, 1970, after a violent altercation that led to the death of patrolman Glenn Edward Smith, Detroit police raided the Panthers' Sixteenth Street headquarters. Hundreds of officers descended upon the headquarters. Police snipers perched on rooftops. Teargas canisters were lobbed into the building. Prepared for what they saw as the inevitable assault, the 15 Panthers outfitted themselves with gas masks and exchanged fire with police using the stockpile of weapons they had amassed. The standoff lasted until shortly before dawn on October 25 when the last Panthers surrendered. At trial, the 15 were acquitted for murder. Three were charged with felonious assault, but followingly successful legal appeals eventually had their sentences overturned. As was the case in other cities across the nation in the early 1970s, legal fees and entanglements with the criminal justice system combined with conflicts between Eldridge Cleaver and Huey P. Newton on the national level to the exhaustion and dismantling of the Detroit's Panthers.

Panthers on the Banks of the Lake Michigan: Milwaukee, Wisconsin

Less than a year after the Detroit chapter of the BPP formed, Booker Collins, Ronald Starks, and Donald Young, all Vietnam War veterans, formed a chapter of the party in Milwaukee in the winter of 1969. Locating their headquarters at 2121 North First Street in the center of Milwaukee's black neighborhood, they opened their doors to community residents seven days per week from noon to 8 pm to assist them in dealing with structural racism, poverty, and brutality. Helping residents was not a theoretical undertaking. Black Milwaukeeans had regularly suffered at the hands of beat patrolmen and rogue officers of the Milwaukee Police Department Tactical Squad. In fact, only two years earlier in late July 1967, this concoction of racism and abuse led African Americans to participate in citywide violence. Fed up with their second-class citizenship, hundreds if not thousands of African Americans rioted for several days. To remedy the ills of hunger throughout the city, Milwaukee Panthers organized a free breakfast program. To protect themselves from police violence, they adopted a self-defensive posture. A member of the fledgling group declared that they would "take no acts of aggression, but we're going to defend ourselves."[2]

Almost as soon as the Milwaukee affiliate was organized, however, police harassment began. In February 1969, the Panthers' deputy minister of defense was embroiled in a violent altercation with police. Months later in June, Nat Bellamy, a local Panther, was arrested and charged with weapons possession after he was injured in an automobile collision with a police cruiser. In August 1969, Richard Smith was detained by police for jaywalking while selling newspapers. Throughout the summer, at least 10 other Panthers were arrested on a variety of weapons charges. On September 22, 1969, Booker Collins, Jesse Lee White, and Earl Walter Leverette were arrested, charged with resisting arrest, and sentenced to a year in jail. The Milwaukee chapter was officially purged by the National Committee in late autumn 1969, because a majority of Milwaukee Panthers were in jail or facing charges and for fear of infiltration by the FBI and other federal and state authorities bent on their destruction.

Between 1970 and the summer of 1973, several former members of the disbanded chapter continued their community work with the free breakfast program at times under the aegis of a branch of the NCCF and at other times under the banner of a new organization, the People's Committee for Survival. In August 1973, the BPP national headquarters gave permission for the restart of an official branch in the city, and with the official sanction, the reconstituted branch engaged the community until it closed again 1977. Panthers filled in potholes, operated a daycare center, ran an egg coop, and worked with other local organizations to improve the lives of African Americans and white working-class Milwaukeeans. By 1974, close to 500 people benefited from the chapter's community programs.

Two of the most important services the Panthers offered were the Busing to Prison Program and the People's Free Medical Clinic (PFMC). For poor people, the cost of visiting incarcerated relatives was financially prohibitive, and for many who did not own a vehicle, a prison visit was often impossible. The Busing to Prison Program was crucial as it allowed family members to remain connected. Initially, Panthers offered weekly bus service from their office in Milwaukee to prisons in Fox Lake, Green Bay, and Waupun, Wisconsin, and at its height, close to 200 people took advantage of the service every week. The high cost associated with the program led the group to scale back its service and offer bus service biweekly, but it remained an important lifeline until the mid-1970s. The PFMC opened in 1970 by former Panthers shortly after the first Milwaukee chapter disbanded. It closed in November 1972, but reopened in the winter of 1973. The PFMC was operated by two paid staff members and white dentists and doctors volunteered their time and expertise at the center and patients received care free of charge. For poor African Americans in the city, the clinic provided health care that could not be obtained either because of the high cost of clinical health services or because facilities were simply unavailable. According to the historian Andrew Witt, the clinic "educated the community on a variety of health issues such as sickle cell anemia, drug abuse, children's health and birth control."[3] The Milwaukee branch officially disbanded in 1977, but throughout the eight years of its operation, the members' political work influenced a generation of activists in the city.

Black Panthers in the Hawkeye State: Des Moines, Iowa

Mary Rhem and Charles Knox organized the Des Moines chapter of the BPP in the summer of 1968, but less than two years later, the Des Moines chapter was expelled by the Central Committee ostensibly for not selling *The Black Panther*, a mandate from headquarters as part of national protocol. At the height of its organizational influence, the group had approximately 100 members working throughout the city's segregated, black Northside neighborhood. Their survival programs varied because the needs of the community varied. Like chapters throughout the nation, Des Moines Panthers organized a free breakfast program that served upward of 100 school-aged children. They applied for and won a grant in the amount of $1,500 from a local antipoverty group and used the money to organize and implement African American social, cultural, and artistic installations and events on University Avenue, the major thoroughfare in black Des Moines. The group also organized literacy programs for its members to teach basic reading and reading comprehension skills to their members who had been underserved by the local public school system. To garner support from white allies, BPP members visited and spoke at Grinnell College, a prestigious private institution, as well as the University of Iowa.

But the Des Moines chapter seems to have been doomed from its start. Only a handful of the 100 members were skilled political organizers, politically savvy, or informed about local or national political developments. A significant number came from the lumpenproletariat, individuals who worked outside the formal economy as drug dealers, hustlers, pimps, and prostitutes, and in other informal jobs. In addition, a sizable number of the membership had no history of political activism and often romanticized the Panthers. Rather than being moved to action by a sense of justice or injustice, many were superficially influenced and motivated by the Black Panthers' signature leather jacket, revolutionary rhetoric, and talk of guns. In Des Moines, members were not properly vetted, and it was suggested by intelligence sources that several Panthers may have planted an incendiary device in late April 1969 that blew apart the city's BPP headquarters and many surrounding homes in hopes of obtaining news coverage. During the fall of 1970, the Des Moines chapter was under increased scrutiny from the Central Committee and had lost the respect of the city's more moderate black and white political leadership. By November 1970, the chapter was expelled. The leaders in California cut off all ties with Des Moines black radicals.

Black Panthers in the Show Me State: Kansas City, Missouri

During the winter and spring of 1968, black activists met in hopes of creating an organization to help remedy some of the problems plaguing African Americans in Kansas City. Among those present at organization meetings were Peter O'Neill, Bill Whitfield, Charlotte Hill, Tommy Robinson, Bill Robinson, Phillip Crayton, Henry Finley, and Andre Rawls. The group's initial name was the Black Vigilantes. They were African Americans dedicated to enforcing the law in their community. In the summer of 1968, the group was granted permission to start a chapter of the BPP, changed its name, and was supervised by the Black Panthers in Illinois.

Kansas City Panthers worked with Panthers in Des Moines, Iowa, and Omaha, Nebraska, on joint projects and rallies but were primarily concerned with sustaining their free breakfast program and their health screening services for sickle cell anemia and hypertension. The group also worked with other local political groups including the National Association for the Advancement of Colored People and the United Fund. When residents asked the Panthers to assist them in vetting programs slotted to air on a local radio station to determine whether they were offensive to listeners, Panthers volunteered their time. The Panthers did not have expertise in radio broadcasting, but they were attuned to point number one of the national platform that called for "power to determine the destiny of our Black Community." In Kansas City in the late 1960s, that political power was at least partially understood to mean the ability to determine who spoke for and about black people on the radio.

The group also embraced point number five of the platform, and used it to respond to the needs of local black Kansas City residents. Point five demanded an "education that teaches us our true history and our role in the present-day society." To that end, the group sponsored political education classes for black and white people interested in joining and supporting the group. Political education for whites was called "Hang the Honkies" parties. During each session, African American history would be taught, beginning with the enslavement of west Africans and end with a discussion of contemporary oppression. According to one member, "the detail[s] would be graphic. Racism was combated by discussion of entitlement to determine our own destiny."[4]

From the organization's beginnings, the chapter was under local police and FBI surveillance. It was infiltrated by undercover agents who sought to obtain information to undermine the Panthers, and these outside forces undoubtedly impacted how the group functioned and affected the number and quality of survival programs offered by the group. However, it was not counterintelligence programs that undermined the Panthers' work; instead, it was a strategic miscalculation by the Panthers that led to them losing community support. In the summer of 1969, John Edward Dacy, a white police officer, was shot and killed. The Panthers were not responsible for his death, but in their public stance, they did not condemn the shooting. For local black and white leaders, it appeared that the young Panthers reveled in the murder. Andre Rawls, one of the founders of the Kansas City chapter and the group's communication secretary penned an article, which appeared in *The Black Panther*, the organization's national newspaper, that glorified Dacy's death. For local black leaders, residents, and white supporters of black progressive politics, celebrating the death of a white police officer was just too much. The Black Panthers lost the respect of the very allies they had cultivated relationships with because of their anti-police/anti-pig rhetoric. The group lumbered along trying to stay afloat for a few more months, but by the winter of 1970, the BPP of Kansas City, Missouri, disbanded and former members found other outlets for their political activity.

Black Panthers in the Cornhusker State: Omaha, Nebraska

Eddie Bolden, a local community activist in Omaha, Nebraska, was given permission by Panthers headquarters to start an Omaha chapter in the summer of 1968. By late fall of 1968, the chapter had a handful of recruits. Two young and eager members, David Rice and Edward Poindexter, became early leaders of the group and started programs to serve the community, including political education classes and armed police patrols, the initial program that made the Oakland chapter so controversial and influential. Internal friction within the group and the nationwide purge in 1969 resulted in the expulsion of the Omaha chapter in August, less than a year from its inception.

Undeterred and wanting to serve the Near North Side, Omaha's black community, Poindexter received permission to organize a NCCF branch. The NCCF rebooted its liberation school and free breakfast program, but by early 1970, vexing troubles revisited the organization. In May, a former Air Force officer was arrested for allegedly attempting to sell stolen munitions to the NCCF. In August, Larry Minard, an Omaha police officer, was killed by a bomb planted by Duane Peak, a 15-year-old member of the branch. Peak declared that David Rice and Edward Poindexter masterminded the plot and a jury believed him. Rice and Poindexter were sentenced to life in prison. During the summer of 1970, the Omaha NCCF was expelled from the party. The party's newspaper declared its expulsion in no uncertain terms in late July when it declared that the "The National Committee to Combat Fascism in Omaha, Nebraska, is no longer functioning as an organizing bureau of the Black Panther Party, or from heretofore connected with the Black Panther Party in anyway."

Notes

1. Ahmad A. Rahman, "Marching Blind: The Rise and Fall of the Black Panther Party in Detroit," in Yohuru Williams and Jama Lazerow, eds., *Liberated Territory: Untold Local Perspectives of the Black Panther Party* (Durham and London: Duke University Press, 2008), 181–231.
2. Andrew Witt, *The Black Panthers in the Midwest: The Community Programs and Services of the Black Panther Party in Milwaukee, 1966–1977*. Kindle edition. (New York: Routledge, 2013), Frame 1182 of 3550.
3. Ibid., Frame of 1441 of 3550.
4. Reynaldo Anderson, "The Kansas City Black Panther Party and the Repression of the Black Revolution," in Judson Jeffries, ed., *On the Ground: The Black Panther Party in Communities across America* (Jackson: University of Mississippi, 2010), 109.

CHAPTER FIVE

The Black
Panthers in Art
and Culture

On February 7, 2016, live in front of tens of thousands of spectators at Levi's Stadium in Santa Clara, California, and televised to millions of viewers throughout the nation and the world, popstar Beyoncé acknowledged the enduring legacy of the Black Panther Party (BPP) in popular culture during her Super Bowl 50 halftime performance. As she performed "Formation," her backup dancers sported the iconic black berets of the BPP. When the performance ended, the dancers posed for pictures giving the clenched fist, Black Power salute. The reference to the BPP was vague to most Americans who never knew, read about, or thought about the BPP, but to those who were Panthers, were influenced by their radical politics, or benefited from the Panthers' social justice and anti-racist work, the performance demonstrated the importance of the organization in popular culture.

One of the earliest film depictions of the Panthers is found in the opening scenes of Michelangelo Antonioni's *Zabriskie Point* (1970).[1] A predominantly white group of leftists discusses the merits and strategies of a student strike they are planning and the meaning of political revolution. Leading the discussion are two black militants: one man and one woman. Neither the militants' names nor their organizational affiliation is revealed, but their style, confrontational strategies, and

Beyoncé performs during the halftime show at Super Bowl 50 at Levi's Stadium in Santa Clara, California, on February 7, 2016. During the performance Beyoncé's dancers raised their fists and gave the black power salute. They also invoked the spirit of the BPP by wearing black leather jackets and berets. (TIMOTHY A. CLARY/AFP/Getty Images)

talk of pigs, fascism, and oppression lead viewers to believe that they are BPP members. It is not clear who the male activist is or whom he supposed to portray, but the woman activist is unmistakably Kathleen Cleaver, Eldridge Cleaver's wife and one of the leaders of the International Section of the BPP. During the boisterous discussion, Cleaver and her black comrade are seen as being more politically savvy and experienced than the white students who, in turn (with some exceptions), look up to them as tried and true revolutionaries. In one fiery exchange between the black militants and the white students, Cleaver's associate notes that: "When a pig busts you on your head, kicking down your door, stopping you from living, when you can't get a job, you can't go to school, you can't eat ... that's what makes you a revolutionary." Antonioni presents the Panthers as part of a larger movement to foment political change for the poor and disfranchised.

Over two decades after Michelangelo Antonioni's *Zabriskie Point* (1970), Robert Zemeckis's award-winning *Forrest Gump* (1994) debuted in mainstream movie theaters. In one scene, Forrest Gump, a decorated Vietnam War veteran, happens upon a meeting of a BPP meeting in Washington, D.C., with Jenny, his childhood friend and her boyfriend, Wesley, the leader of Students for a Democratic Society (SDS) in Berkeley, California. Throughout the scene, BPP members in black berets and black leather jackets are frantically planning their strategy to protect their leaders from violence and their communities from oppression. They move haphazardly and loudly around a make-shift headquarters, espousing their revolutionary rhetoric to a captive audience. When Wesley strikes Jenny across the face, Forrest comes to her aid. He tackles Wesley, and then continues to punch him while Wesley lay on the ground. Forrest only stops after Jenny's repeated requests for him to do so while BPP members stand around, unable or unwilling to intervene. When the brawl is concluded, Forrest and Jenny quietly leave and enter the dark night. The Black Panthers are a punch line in *Forrest Gump*: gunslingers with pistols that do not shoot.

One should not be surprised by the contrasting film depictions. The two directors were operating and creating art in very different political and cultural climates. Antonioni directed his movie in the politically progressive times of the late 1960s. For him, the BPP was a revolutionary force trying to change the lives of black Americans and eradicate racism and classism. Zemeckis's *Forrest Gump* was conceived, written, filmed, and produced in a period following a white, conservative backlash and projected white America's fear of the BPP during its heyday and a continued fear of the black political activity in the 1990s. Academic Jane Rhodes offers a convincing argument about Zemeckis's portrayal of the Panthers in her book *Framing the Black Panthers: The Spectacular Rise of a Black Power Icon*. In it she notes: "[Zemeckis's] portrayal of the Panthers as hate-filled, unstable, and politically bereft ... [fuels] a historical memory that lies somewhere between ridicule and condemnation."[2]

Mario Van Peebles's film *Panther* (1995) is an adaption of his father's novel by the same name and is the most popular cinema rendering of the organization.[3] Its cast is phenomenal. Courtney B. Vance, the stage, television, and film actor, plays the role of Bobby Seale. Marcus Chong, a stellar actor, is Huey P. Newton. Anthony Griffith is Eldridge Cleaver. Bokeem Woodbine plays a steadfast Panther recruiter and foot soldier. Kadeem Hardison, a popular television actor in the late 1980s and early 1990s plays Judge, the main character. He is a black Vietnam War veteran and college student at the University of California, Berkeley. The film dramatizes the origins and early development of the party through Judge's eyes. At Newton's request, Judge acts as an informant for the police to provide misinformation, which causes friction within the party. Throughout the film, young Panther black men and women are fighting against police brutality and racism in California's Bay Area and are also victims of state-sponsored oppression. State and federal law enforcement, intimidation, subterfuge, violence, and drugs in black ghettos throughout the nation are responsible for the demise of the Panthers. Peebles's *Panther* is a loose reading of history and provides a sympathetic cinematic account of the Panthers' history. In an interview about the film, Peebles declared that "We've had plenty of time to see their [white] heroes; when are we going to canonize us?" For Peebles, members of the BPP were and continue to be heroes in black communities throughout the nation.

Peebles was part of a larger creative class of black artists, including hip-hop musicians, who possessed a renewed interest in black radicalism in general and the BPP in particular during the late 20th century. Throughout the hip-hop world, artists encouraged a younger generation to (re)consider the Panthers' message. None were more adroit and outspoken at this time than Oscar Jackson, Jr., otherwise known as Paris. Paris was and continues to be a gifted director, producer, song writer, and performer. In 1990, he released *The Devil Made Me Do It* with Tommy Boy Records.[4] The Tommy Boy Record label signed some of the most important hip-hop artists of the 1990s, including, but not limited to, De La Soul, Prince Paul, and Queen Latifah. In *The Devil Made Me Do It*, Paris saw his creative endeavors in the 1990s as directly related to the work of the Panthers in the 1960s and 1970s. On the first track of the album, "Intro," he connects the 1989 killing of Yusef Hawkins, a 16-year-old African American teenager killed by a white mob in the Bensonhurst neighborhood of Brooklyn, New York, to the 1968 shooting of Bobby Hutton, a 17-year-old and one of the founding members of the party. Paris quotes Bobby Seale in "Intro": "Black people are now to organize in a fashion where we have maximum retaliation against all forms of racist, police brutality and attacks."

In the song "Panther Power," Paris cites the BPP's Ten Point Platform to oppose police brutality in the 1990s and calls for black people to protect their community. It begins with a quote by Bobby Seale: "So the concept is this, basically: The whole black nation has to be put together as a black army and we're going to walk on this nation. We're going to walk on this racist power structure. And we're going to say to the whole damn government, Stick 'em up, mother**ker. This is a hold-up! We come for what's ours!" It ends with a mantra of the party: "The Revolution Has Come. Off the Pigs. It's time to pick up the Gun. Off the Pig!" "On the Prowl" is a short mix of a hip-hop beat, with a black panther growling, with a police siren in background. "Brutal" provides a layperson's account of the African American freedom struggle and connects the founding of the Nation of Islam and the rise of Malcolm with the founding of the BPP. "Escape from Babylon" repeats the entire Ten Point Program of the party.

Two years after his first album, in 1992, Paris released *Sleeping with the Enemy*.[5] Because of its politically contested content and lyrics, he released the album on his own label, Scareface Records. If one questioned Paris's real or supposed link to or veneration of the Panthers, one only needs to listen to "Make Way for a Panther." In no uncertain terms, Paris is a Panther and has inherited a revolutionary movement: "the revolutionary has to be wise ... not for the sake that he wants live ... but that the revolution may live and thrive." In "Guerillas in the Mist" he is still "anti-pig." "Assata's Song" is a tribute to Assata Shakur, a Black Panther who was questionably convicted of murder, incarcerated in the state of New Jersey, escaped prison, and found haven in Cuba. Both *The Devil Made Me Do It* and *Sleeping with the Enemy* possess all the hallmarks of many 1990s' hip-hop albums with their homophobic language, self-promotion, and, to some degree, political naiveté. However, the takeaway is that Paris kept the Black Panthers' politics alive in African American cultural production.

Polygram Records released *Pump Ya Fist* three years after *Sleeping with the Enemy*, in 1995.[6] The album was subtitled *Hip Hop Inspired by the Black Panther Party* and it features some of the most important contemporary voices in the hip-hop industry, including Rakim, KRS One, and the Fugees. The musicians rarely reference the BPP, the Panthers' political stances, or the Panthers' ideology, but all of the songs possess the spirit of Panthers' in a post-civil rights movement era and post-Black Power movement era. For example, in "Pump Ya

Fist," the rapper and recording artist Kam asks the listener: "if you hate seeing black peopled get dissed, then pump ya fist." Surely, the language used to describe African Americans' plight has changed and the medium by which ideas are expressed (i.e., hip hop), but the frustration with black poverty and police brutality has not.

In 2000, Common released his song "A Song for Assata," an ode to Assata Shakur, a Black Panther who was jailed for the murder of a New Jersey state trooper, on his *Like Water for Chocolate* album.[7] In it, Common retells Assata Shakur's detention, describes her experience with police brutality, and highlights her struggle for black freedom and justice. The album includes Assata's voice when Common visited her in Cuba, where she was self-exiled after her prison break in the late 1970s. "Freedom! You askin' me about freedom ... freedom is the right to grow, is the right to blossom. Freedom is—is the right to be yourself, to be who you are."

As recently as 2015, *The New York Times*, one of the most respected news organizations in the world, featured a short documentary directed by Zackary Canepari and Ora Dekornfeld.[8] In it, the Grammy Award–winning rhythm and blues artist D'Angelo has a conversation with Bobby Seale. Together, they explore the roots and strategies of the BPP as they cruise around the San Francisco Bay Area in a vintage convertible. Canepari and Dekornfeld allow the viewer to see Bobby Seale as an elderly revolutionary statesman alongside one of the originators of the black neo-soul music movement of the late 20th and early 21st century. In the 4 minutes and 22-second documentary, we conclude that 50 years after its founding, the BPP was influenced by black musicians of their time and that the party continues to influence black music and black urban politics in modern times.

Unlike Peebles's *Panther* or Common's "Assata," Tanya Hamilton's *Night Catches Us* (2010)[9] does not claim to be an official or unofficial history; instead, it is a fictional rendering of the BPP in Philadelphia after the party's heyday. The film won numerous nominations and awards including the Audience Award at the 2010 New Orleans Film Festival. It presents no heroic renderings, just portraits of former BPP in a north Philadelphia neighborhood in the mid-1970s. Marcus, played by Anthony Mackie, is a former Panther who returns to his old neighborhood to attend his father's funeral after having been gone for several years. He was forced to leave the city for fears that he would be killed

Common at the 2016 MTV Movie Awards in Burbank, California. Common is one of many hip-hop musicians influenced by the BPP and has spoken about them in his music. (Starstock /Dreamstime)

by ex-Panthers for informing on his friend and Panther comrade, Neal, who was killed by the police after they raided his home, suspecting that he had killed a police officer. Neale, Iris's (Jamara Griffin) father, was married to Patricia, Iris's mother, former Panther, and community lawyer played by Kerry Washington. Patricia is haunted by her husband's death and attempts to balance her work life and motherhood. Iris is a curious and brooding nine-year-old who tries to learn about her father, about whom no one speaks. Throughout the film, the audience sees all characters trying to make sense of their particular relationship with the party. In the end, we are left with an image of a local party chapter that lost its way with individual members and supporters trying to make sense of that legacy.

Rather than being an organization that helped the community through survival programs, it became an organization concerned only with vengeance. After the police killed two panthers, Neal and others decided to kill a police officer. This decision caused stress in Neal and Patricia's marriage. The stress became so great that Patricia, not Marcus, informed on Neal, for fear of her safety and Iris's well-being. Fear of violent reprisal and police corruption forced Marcus out of his neighborhood for good. Iris was left without a father and few male role models. Jimmy followed Neal's path: he killed a police officer and was eventually shot dead after a manhunt.

Spike Lee directed *The Huey P. Newton Story* (2001),[10] an adaptation of Roger Guenveur Smith's 1996 Obie Award–winning, off-Broadway, one-man show of the same name. *The Huey P. Newton Story* features Smith as Newton who presents his (auto)biography to a live audience and contains contemporary images and sound clips from the late 1960s and early 1970s. Throughout the film/play, Newton is presented as a chain smoking, self-reflective theorist, poet, and cultural critic who easily quotes from sources as varied as sacred scriptures, Shakespeare, and Paul Robeson, the African American activist and artist. The audience learns of Newton's upbringing, influences, imprisonment, and political organizing. It is obvious that Smith did his research on Newton, but the viewer must be clear that *The Huey P. Newton Story*, like all other Hollywood renderings of the party, is a work of fiction and not meant to be a historically accurate portrayal of Newton or the party. Nonetheless, one gets a dramatic glimpse of a man who changed African American history and the politics of the United States.

The Panthers make a brief appearance in Kevin Rodney Sullivan's comedy *Barbershop 2* (2004)[11] and Lee Daniels's *The Butler* (2013).[12] *Barbershop 2* tells the story of how Calvin (played by Ice-Cube), a second-generation African American barber, tries to maintain and grow the South Side Chicago shop he inherited from his father. In one scene, Eddie, an older African American barber who worked with Calvin's father, reminisces about the shop and its role in black politics of the 1970s. The scene is short: after being driven from their headquarters by police tear gas, the Chicago-based Black Panthers enter the barber shop with Eddie, the barber who is at best a tangential member. The leader of the group addresses the staff and customers of the barbershop, informing them that the Panthers will continue to serve the people through their community service programs. Eddie, all the while stands on the side, unsure, unconvinced, and unnerved when the Panther leaders talk about how the police may ambush the group with guns and how the group will defend themselves with guns when necessary. When they exit the shop, Eddie declares that the group was "crazy." The BPP is an effectual joke in U.S. and Chicago's history. Rather than being presented as a political organization seeking to improve economic and political opportunities for black people, the BPP is the butt of the joke in a film created, directed, and produced for black people, the very people the BPP sought to help.

Based on the life of Eugene Allen, *The Butler* tells the story of Cecil Gaines (played by Forest Whitaker), a butler in the White House in Washington, D.C. Gaines serves in his position during the politically tumultuous decades of the mid-20th century. As African Americans' search for freedom expands in the 1950s and 1960s, Gaines's son Louis (played by David Oyelowo) joins the movement. He is part of the Freedom Rides in the early 1960s, joins Martin Luther King, Jr.'s Southern Christian Leadership Conference, and then, after King's assassination, joins the BPP. For Louis, the Panthers are a natural extension of the struggle for civil rights, but it is also an organization that has lost its way. Rather than focusing on community service and serving the people, the young revolutionaries were bent on avenging the death of their comrades by killing white police officers. For the FBI and Richard Nixon's administration, the Panthers are a menace that needed to be neutralized. Dismayed, Louis leaves the Panthers.

The Panthers were a political force to be reckoned with during their time. Not only did they challenge political authority and shock Americans' imagination of what and who black people were, but they continued to challenge Americans' imaginations through popular culture well after their organizational demise.

Notes

1. *Zabriskie Point.* Directed by Michelangelo Antonioni. Beverly Hills, California: Metro-Goldwyn-Mayer, 1970.

2. Jane Rhodes, *Framing the Black Panthers: The Spectacular Rise and Fall of a Black Power Icon* (New York: The New Press, 2007), 29.

3. *Panther*. Directed by Mario Van Peebles. Universal City, California: Gramercy Pictures, 1995.

4. Paris. *The Devil Made Me Do It*. Tommy Boy Records TBCD-10301990, 1990 compact disc.

5. Paris. *Sleeping with the Enemy*. Scareface Records SCR007-100-1, 1992 vinyl.

6. *Pump Ya Fist: Hip Hop Inspired by the Black Panther*. Polygram 314 527 609-2, 1995 compact disc.

7. Common, *Like Water for Chocolate*. MCA Records 088 111 970-1, 2000, vinyl.

8. "Black Panther Professor: Bobby Seale and D'Angelo in Oakland," *The New York Times*. https:/www.youtube.com/watch?v=72Dfp-PzOLE.

9. *Night Catches Us*. Directed by Tanya Hamilton. New York: Simonsays Entertainment, 2010.

10. *The Huey P. Newton Story*. Directed by Spike Lee. New York: 40 Acres and a Mule Filmworks, 2001.

11. *Barbershop 2 Back in Business*. Directed by Kevin Rodney Sullivan. Beverly Hills, California: Metro-Goldwyn-Mayer, 2004.

12. *The Butler*. Directed by Lee Daniels. New York: The Weinstein Company, 2013.

Conclusion

By the early 1970s, the Central Committee in Oakland, California, had put down the bullet in favor of the ballot and had Bobby Seale run for the mayoralty in Oakland. The move was a measured response to what was happening nationally and a practical political move to stay viable in at least one city. Counterintelligence measures by federal, state, and local law enforcement had taken its toll on chapters and affiliates nationwide. As Black Panther Party (BPP) members were jailed as political prisoners and for actual criminal acts, it became increasingly difficult for chapters and the Central Committee to raise and use funds to make bail for those arrested and pay for lengthy, politically motivated trials. Also, with Eldridge Cleaver's expulsion from the party in February 1971, a clear split in the organization was made clear. There were those who supported Cleaver who believed in and supported armed revolutionary struggle against imperialism and capitalism, on the one hand. Cleaver's supporters were summarily expelled or resigned from their posts to join other organizations. On the other hand, there were those who supported and followed Huey P. Newton, who, while not completely opposed to armed struggle, favored the creation and expansion of survival programs in black communities nationwide.

Perhaps the reason why the Central Committee switched to electoral politics, the ballot, is because it recognized that by the early 1970s black people believed in the power of electoral politics. They had seen black men become mayor of major cities. Carl Stokes was the first African American mayor of a major city when he was elected in 1967 in Cleveland, Ohio. Coleman Young was elected mayor of Detroit, Michigan, in 1970. In 1973, Maynard Jackson was elected mayor of Atlanta, Georgia. In 1968, the nation saw Shirley Chisholm run for and win her New York congressional seat, becoming the first African American woman to serve in Congress. Four years later, they watched her take on special interest groups and the Democratic Party establishment to run for president of the United States. While she was not elected to serve as president, she succeeded in highlighting issues of gender and racial discrimination.

The majority of black people in the 1970s were not going to use the bullet to obtain their constitutional rights or economic mobility, and BPP leaders knew this. Consequently, rather than tear down the system, the party would work within existing political and economic system, reform it, and make it work for all people. It decided to close chapters and branches, bring all Panthers to Oakland, participate in voter registration drives, and work to get Bobby Seale elected the first black mayor of Oakland. During Bobby Seale's mayoral campaign, the Panthers organized several high-profile community programs. One of the first and most important in galvanizing support was the Black Community Survival Conference held from March 29 to March 30, 1972. The advertisement in the *Black Panther* informed readers and potential attendees that "10,000 Free Bags of Groceries with chickens in every bag will be given away."[1]

Seale, having been a stand-up comedian, was a gregarious candidate and often met voters in community centers, on city buses, and on the street. He did not win his bid for mayor, but he laid the foundation for Lionel Wilson who became the first black mayor of Oakland and served consecutive terms from 1977 to 1991; Elihu Harris, the second African American mayor of Oakland who served from 1991 to 1999; and Ronald V. Dellums, the third African American mayor of Oakland who served from 2007 to 2011. Arguably, he also laid the foundation for the first Asian American woman, Jean Quan (2011–2015), and the first white woman, Libby Schaaf, to serve as

Bobby Seale, political activist and cofounder of the Black Panthers, speaks to a crowd of approximately 250, after his arraignment at Berkeley County Court-house, February 1968. (Bettmann/Getty)

mayor (2015–present) by challenging traditional racial politics in the city and offering a progressive platform that appealed to broad segments of the city's multicultural electorate. Seale's influence on electoral politics is indicative of the BPP's legacy.

In the United States, the Young Lords, the Gray Panthers, and the Yellow Power Movement were all influenced by the BPP. In the late 1960s and early 1970s, the Panthers' work encouraged the Young Lords, a revolutionary Puerto Rican liberation party, to work on behalf of the Puerto Rican people on the Island of Puerto Rico and in the Puerto Rican diaspora fight for the liberation of all oppressed people. The Gray Panthers were founded by retired women in the early 1970s and per-severed throughout the late 20th century as "an organization of intergen-erational activists working to change laws and attitudes for social and economic justice. Some of the many issues they have tackled include peace, health care, jobs, housing, ageism, sexism, racism, media stereo-typing, family security, the environment and campaign reform."[2] Reporter Nadra Kareem Nittle notes that "The 'black power' movement caused many Asian Americans to question themselves," and that "Yellow power," in 1968 "was at the stage of an articulated mood rather than a program—disillusionment and alienation from white America and independence, race pride and self-respect."[3] Put simply, the BPP's changing political ideologies and internationalism put the party in contact with communities of color, communities of progressive whites, and individuals across the nation and the world who were trying to make sense of their lives and their abilities to affect positive change in their lives.

Historians Michael L. Clemons and Charles E. Jones have noted the international influence of the Panthers. "Both Black Britons and White activists in England, respectively, formed organizations patterned on the BPP. The Black Panther Movement and the White Panthers of the United Kingdom represented British manifestations of the Panther phenomenon." They also note that "the BPP ... inspired Oriental Jews in Israel, Aborigines in Australia, and members of the 'untouchable' class in India to form insurgent organizations modeled on the Black Panther Party."[4] The Black Panther Movement was founded in England in 1968. The Black Cadre was organized in Bermuda in 1969. The White Panthers of the United Kingdom was established in 1970. The Black Panther Party of Israel was founded in 1971. The Black Panther Party of Australia was created in 1972, and the Dalit Panthers of India was established in 1972. In their 1973 Dalit Panther manifest, Bombay, India, Panthers declared that "[d]ue to the hideous plot of American imperialism, the Third Dalit World, that is, oppressed nations, and Dalit people are suffering ... To meet the force of reaction and remove this exploitation, the Black Panther movement grew. From the Black Panthers, Black Power emerged ... We claim a close relationship with this struggle."[5] Nico Slate, the noted historian of African American international politics, has noted that in the southwestern Pacific nation of New Zealand, Polynesian Panthers "wielded the Panther image toward very local ends like unmasking the brutality of settler colonialism and forging a racial conception of indigenous solidarity."[6]

The Panthers' political work has had unintended consequences and as it influenced the rise of an organization that uses its name, but not its motives, political ideologies, or broad organizing strategies. The New Black Panther Party for Self Defense (NBPP) was established in Dallas, Texas, in 1989, as a black nationalist and Pan-African political organization. By taking on the name of the original Panthers, the NBPP sees itself as furthering the mission of Huey P. Newton, Bobby Seale, and all the young men and women who struggled for African American dignity and equality during the 1960s and 1970s. The NBPP uses language of the original Panthers in their platform, and it is clear that the NBPP cares about the lives of black people, racism, and black exploitation.[7] However, its Afrocentrism, cultural nationalism, and reliance on the teachings of Marcus Garvey's Universal Negro Improvement Association and Elijah Muhammad's Nation of Islam sound more like the cultural nationalists that the BPP opposed rather than its Marxist-Leninist and anti-racist stances.

It was clear from their beginnings that the NBPP was and continues to be a fringe group in African Americans' continuing work for justice and equality. However, their emergence was troubling for some. The Huey P. Newton Foundation, an organization that devoted itself to maintaining the legacy of the BPP and cofounded by Huey P. Newton's wife, Fredericka Newton, rejected the NBPP. In a 2009 statement, the foundation maintained that "[t]here is no New Black Panther Party," and that the NBPP has "no legitimate claim on the party's name" and "only pretends to walk in the footsteps of the party's true heroes."[8]

The Huey P. Newton Foundation was not the only organization that has opposed the NBPP. The Southern Poverty Law Center, a social justice advocacy and educational organization, declared that the "New Black Panther Party is a virulently racist and anti-Semitic organization whose leaders have encouraged violence against whites, Jews and law enforcement officers."[9] The Anti-Defamation League called the NBPP "the largest organized anti-Semitic and racist Black militant group in America."[10]

In the early 21st century, the BPP has been and continues to have significant historical and political importance to many people in the United States. In October 2001, former Panthers, scholars, and activists assembled to reassess, reevaluate, and reconceptualize the history and legacy of the BPP at the University of the District of Columbia for the 35th anniversary of the founding of the BPP. Two years later, in June 2003, at Wheelock College in Boston, Massachusetts, historians Jama Lazerow and Yohuru Williams organized the Black Panther Party in Historical Perspective Conference. In October 2014, the Black Panther Commemoration Committee in New York City and the New York–based Maysles Documentary Cinema organized a BPP film festival in Harlem, New York. That same month, there was a BPP legacy celebration that remembered and recognized the BPP nationwide and the local Kansas City Panther group in Kansas City, Missouri. In September 2016, organizers successfully held the Seattle Black Panther Party Revolutionary Film Festival and Forum in Seattle, Washington, which included a presentation by Aaron Dixon, the former BPP captain, and Terika Lewis, one of the many black women who joined the party and kept it focused on serving the people. These events offered opportunities for former Panthers to tell their stories and for people to learn more about the history of the party.

Over the last decade, scholars have been very interested in (re) writing the history of the BPP on the national and local levels. Their work has revealed the particular ways in which the BPP appealed to African Americans and white Americans in cities throughout the nation. Their writing has also shown how members, individual chapters, and affiliates effectively negotiated local politics to develop into meaningful and vibrant political actors and organization as was the case in New Haven, Connecticut, or ineffectively as was the case in Omaha, Nebraska, which failed to serve local African American residents.

If we define "counterculture" as "a culture and values and mores that run counter to those of established society," then the BPP and its members were countercultural. In the mid- to late 1960s, when Newton and Seale created the BPP, broad swathes of the white population from all political persuasions and economic status viewed black people as inferior, or at least people they should not concern themselves with. The BPP opposed racism in a society where structural, institutional, and interpersonal racism were normalized. Cornel West, the renowned African American theologian and philosopher, notes that the BPP was a "visionary group of young Black people [who] decided to highlight the fundamental pillar of white supremacy and antidemocratic practice against Black people—namely, the vicious and unaccountable repressive actions of white police power over Black folk."[11] Most importantly,

A teacher leads his students with the black power salute and slogans at a Black Panther liberation school, San Francisco, December 1969. (Bettmann/Getty)

in an era when African Americans were assumed to have achieved their basic constitutional rights, the BPP stood firm to remind black people and the nation that despite the gains of the civil rights movement, social, economic, and political equality was not a reality for large segments of African Americans and more needed to be done locally and nationally.

Notes

1. "10,000 Free Bags of Groceries," *The Black Panther*, March 11, 1972, p. 9.
2. http://www.pbs.org/independentlens/maggiegrowls/panthers.html. Accessed July 11, 2017.
3. http://www.thoughtco.com/asian-american-civil-rights-movement-history-2834596. Accessed July 11, 2017.
4. Kathleen Cleaver and George Katsiaficas, eds., *Liberation, Imagination, and the Black Panther Party* (New York: Routledge, 2001), 23.
5. Bryan Shih and Yohuru Williams, *The Black Panthers: Portraits from an Unfinished Revolution* (New York: Nation Books, 2016), 79.
6. Ibid., 80.
7. See The New Black Panther Party, Ten Point Platform in the primary documents section.

8. http://www.washingtontimes.com/news/2009/nov/16/black-panthers-denounce-new-panthers/.

9. https://edit.splcenter.org/fighting-hate/extremist-files/group/new-black-panther-party.

10. https:/www.adl.org/sites/default/files/documents/assets/pdf/anti-semitism/united-states/new-black-panther-party-for-self-defense-2014-11-21.pdf.

11. David Hilliard, *The Black Panther Party Service to the People Programs* (Albuquerque: University of New Mexico Press, 2008), ix.

Biographical Sketches

Huey P. Newton (1942–1989)

Huey P. Newton was a leader and cofounder of the Black Party for
Self Defense. Named after the Louisiana senator Huey Long, Newton
was the seventh child of Armelia and Walter Newton in Monroe,
Louisiana. At age three, Huey P. Newton migrated to Oakland,
California, with his family, searching for economic opportunity and a
better quality of life. During the years following World War II, Oakland
boasted a burgeoning African American population and a busy port that
promised more possibilities than Louisiana ever could. For the Newton
family and other black families like them, however, Oakland was not
the Promised Land: schools were substandard, living accommodations
were meager, at best, and jobs were ephemeral.

Melvin Newton and Walter "Sonny Man" Newton Jr., Newton's
two older brothers, and Walter Newton, Sr., Newton's father, were
most influential in Newton's childhood development. Melvin epito-
mized the potential of pursuing a life of ideas. He attended San Jose
State College and taught his brother Huey the value of learning.
"Sonny Man," leaving home as a teenager, thrived in the illegal
economy and showed Huey the allure of street life. Huey P. Newton

would later recall that while Sonny Man appeared to live freely, this freedom was only an illusion. Despite the illusion, Walter provided Huey P. Newton with lessons to negotiate life on Oakland's streets. To Huey, Newton Sr. was the glue that held their family together. Holding multiple jobs and performing the duties of a Christian minister, Walter Newton Sr. combined spirituality with pragmatism and taught his sons the necessity of opposing white racism.

Never feeling at home in structured classrooms, Newton received his education during his formative years on the streets of Oakland. There he and his friends experimented with, acted out, and constantly engaged the politics of masculinity and found the hustler's life appealing. In the 10th grade at Oakland Technical High School, Newton was expelled for his behavior and he transferred to Berkeley High School in Berkeley, California. Newton's experience at Berkeley High School was only a little better. In fact, it was at Berkeley High School that Newton's trouble with the law began, forcing him to go to juvenile hall. Unable to attend Berkeley High School upon leaving juvenile hall, Newton returned to Oakland Technical High School and graduated in 1959.

Social promotion and the politics of bureaucratic public high schools allowed Newton to graduate without possessing the requisite scholastic aptitude. After a period of self-directed study under the tutelage of his brother Melvin, however, Newton entered Oakland City College in the autumn of 1959. It was at Oakland City College from 1959 to 1966 that Newton began actively seeking answers to the problems plaguing African American communities nationwide. Reading radical theorists like Che Guevara, Malcolm X, Frantz Fanon, Karl Marx, and Mao Zedong, and participating in black cultural and political organizations, Newton began to develop his own theoretical framework. The first organizations he joined while in college were the Afro-American Association and the Soul Students Advisory Council, student groups devoted to studying African American history, political thought, and cultural production, and creating black studies curriculum on campus. Disappointed with the presence of political consciousness, but lack of political activity in the two organizations, especially the two groups' dismissal of black working poor men, Huey P. Newton and Bobby Seale, a friend and fellow student at Oakland City College, created the Black Panther Party.

The Black Panthers were initially organized in 1966 as an armed police patrol to protect black community residences from brutal police violence. By 1969, with Bobby Seale as its chairman and Huey P. Newton as its minister of self-defense, the organization went nationwide, with more than 40 chapters devoted to the daily concerns of black urban communities.

In autumn 1967, Newton's life took a dramatic turn when a police traffic stop became deadly. Newton had been a victim of police harassment since his days of police patrols in 1967. After being pulled over for unknown circumstances in the early morning hours of October 28, 1967, an altercation with the police left Patrolman John Frey dead, Patrolman Herbert Heanes wounded, and Newton near death with a bullet in his stomach. Treated for his bullet wounds at Kaiser Hospital, Newton was interrogated, brutalized, and chained to a gurney by police. Newton retained the services of Charles Garry, a prominent lawyer known for working with leftist causes. Accused of murder, felonious assault, and kidnapping, Newton awaited trial in San Quentin Prison and Oakland County Jail. After months on trial, on September 8, 1968, Newton was found guilty of manslaughter and sentenced to two to fifteen years sentence at the California Men's Colony, East Facility, in San Luis Obsipo, California. Most of Newton's 22 months

Members of the Black Panther Party march in New York City to protest the murder trial of Huey P. Newton, July 22, 1968. (Bettmann/Getty)

at the penal colony were spent in isolation. While Newton was imprisoned, Charles Garry feverishly worked to obtain an appeal. On May 28, 1970, the California Appellate Court announced that Newton's conviction was reversed and determined that, because the jury had been denied critical information in determining Newton's fate, a new trial was ordered. In August 1970, Newton was released on bail. In the early 1970s, Newton's legal defense team participated in two more trials to save him from imprisonment. Both ended in a mistrial. Cleared of all charges, Newton set out to rebuild the party.

The Federal Bureau of Investigation's Counterintelligence Program (COINTELPRO) from 1970 to 1974, however, made bolstering the party difficult. Also, Newton's move to possess absolute authority over the party, going by names like supreme commander, the servant of the people, and the supreme servant of the people, made strengthening the party difficult. Furthermore, Newton's stardom among the country's celebrities, who provided him with luxury items, drugs, and alcohol, compromised his position among those individuals the party purported to serve.

Newton's drug abuse and alcoholism may have contributed to his fleeing the county in 1974 and further estranged the Black Panther Party (BPP) from black communities. In late 1973, Newton allegedly shot a prostitute, Kathleen Smith, and brutalized a tailor, Preston Callins, for calling him "baby." Shortly after being arrested and posting bail for assaulting Callins, Newton fled the United States and obtained asylum in Cuba where he remained until 1977, relinquishing control of the declining BPP to Elaine Brown. Upon his return to the United States, Newton was imprisoned, released on bail, and eventually acquitted for the murder of Smith. Callins's case was dropped after he declared that he could not remember his assaulter. Newton also resumed control of the party after Elaine Brown resigned her post, citing irreconcilable differences with Newton.

After the BPP officially disbanded in 1982, Newton's wife, Fredericka, left him, and his drug and alcohol abuse, as well as his problems with law enforcement, continued. In 1985, he was suspected of, but never indicted for, burglary. In 1986, he was cleared of possessing illegal firearms. In 1988, Newton served time in prison for parole violation. On August 22, 1989, Newton was fatally wounded after being shot three times in what seems to have been a drug deal gone awry.

Despite COINTELPRO initiatives created by the FBI to discredit Newton, Newton's involvement with the criminal justice system, his authoritarianism within the party, and his drug problems, especially during the last decade of his life, Huey P. Newton was a scholar and the BPP's chief theoretician. In 1966, after six years of study, Newton received his associate's degree. In 1974, he earned a bachelor's degree in education and politics from the University of California, Santa Cruz. In 1980, he obtained his doctorate from the History of Consciousness Program at the University of California, Santa Cruz, by successfully defending his dissertation "War against the Panthers: A Study of Repression in America."

Interestingly, although graduating high school with substandard educational skills, Newton was a prolific writer who (co)authored five books and scores of articles, essays, and position papers. These writings are indicative of Newton's openness to ideas, his ability to synthesize political theories, and a willingness to develop his own understanding of the oppressive forces and strategies to eliminate structural inequalities that jeopardized African Americans' social, political, and economic well-being.

In 1966, when the party was initially organized, Newton was a black nationalist and posited that only black people's control of capitalist institutions in their communities could bring about African American empowerment. In 1969, Newton's understanding of Marxism led him to embrace revolutionary socialism as an ideology necessary to seize economic and political power from the elite ruling class and end the exploitation of the poor and working classes. By 1970, Newton hypothesized that only an internationalist struggle linking radical and progressive forces in different countries could bring about fundamental change. In 1971, Newton's intercommunalism combined ideas of empire and imperialism to articulate an understanding of social movements that transcended the confines of national boundaries.

Newton's political growth and demise were symptomatic of the shifts in the U.S. post–civil rights era political economy. In the 1970s, the most ostensible constraints on African Americans' well-being were apparently removed with 1960s' civil rights legislation, the end of white mob rule, and the ascendance of neoconservative ideologists who coopted notions of equal protection. Heterogeneous black working-class communities that had been created only decades before were floundering under burdens of northern racism, capitalist exploitation, and black people's search for cultural and political identity. Newton's ideological and political development and ultimate ruin is indicative of the hope, potential, and reality of progressive factions in American society who challenged systems of oppression and exploitation. Huey P. Newton may not fit the American fantasy of a spotless, pure hero, but he does epitomize the complex nature of the radical liberation movements in a global age.

Bobby Seale (1936–)

Born Roger George Seale, Bobby Seale was one of the founders of the Black Panther Party in 1966. Seale was born in Dallas, Texas, in the throes of the Great Depression and traveled around the state with his family until they relocated to Berkeley, California, in the mid-1940s. He was educated in San Francisco Bay Area's segregated public school system and managed to graduate from Berkeley High School.

In 1955, he enlisted in the U.S. Air Force. Several years later, in 1959, he was dishonorably discharged when he repeatedly failed to follow the commands of a superior officer. After his discharge, Seale took classes at Merritt College, formerly San Francisco State—Oakland City College, for several years. It was there that his politicization began with two student groups: the Afro-American Association, a black nationalist group; and the Soul Students Advisory Committee. The groups forced the Merritt College administrators to create and expand a black studies curriculum, hire faculty of color, and improve recruitment and retention of students. Finding the student groups' focus to be politically limited, Seale and his new friend, Huey P. Newton, set out to create an organization that dealt with the needs of Oakland's black community. In 1966, they formed the Black Panther Party for Self Defense, with Seale as the chairman and Newton as the minister for self-defense.

Seale worked as a part-time comic and used his speaking ability to encourage young people in Oakland and throughout the nation to rally against injustice. Such charisma, however, put him at odds with local, state, and federal law enforcement, especially the Federal Bureau of Investigation who used its counterintelligence program to paint Seale and the Panthers as a hate group. On May 2, 1967, he led a contingent of armed members to Sacramento, California, the seat of the state government, to oppose the Mulford Act, proposed legislation aimed at stripping the Panthers of their right to bear arms. At the state capitol, he read the Black Panther Executive Mandate #1. The mandate read in part that "The Black Panther Party for Self Defense believes that the time has come for Black People to arm themselves against this terror before it is too late."[1] He was arrested and charged with carrying a concealed weapon. The charges were later dropped. On February 25, 1968, in Berkeley, California, police raided Seale's home without a warrant and charged him and his wife, Artie, with conspiracy to commit murder. In early 1969, Seale and seven other defendants were indicted by a grand jury in Chicago, Illinois, for conspiracy to incite riots during the 1968 Democratic National Convention. During the trial in fall 1969, Seale insisted on representing himself, but the judge refused and had court officers bound and gag him for the duration of the trial. He was found guilty of multiple counts of contempt of court and was sentenced to four years in prison, a sentence that was eventually dismissed. In August 1969, he was arrested and charged with ordering the murder of Alex Rackley in New Haven, Connecticut. After a lengthy trial and imprisonment in Connecticut, he was found not guilty in 1971.

In May 1972, Seale began his bid for mayor of Oakland. Oakland was to be the beginning of a series of successful, local electoral bids throughout the nation wherein political progressives and Black Panthers would ascend to office and implement policies and practices to benefit working-class people and people of color. In response, Panthers from around the country closed their offices and descended upon the city to assist Seale in his political campaign. Seale's bid was encouraged by Congresswoman Shirley Chisholm's presidential campaign, and unlike Eldridge Cleaver's presidential campaign in 1968, Seale presented himself as a viable candidate who effectively challenged the incumbent Mayor John Reading. With no clear winner after the initial election, Seale and Reading were forced to conduct a run-off. Reading received 77,476 votes. Seale received 43,719 votes, close to 40 percent of the city vote.

There is conflicting information as to when Seale left the BPP. Some sources suggest that he was expelled by Huey P. Newton who, by 1973, had become increasingly erratic in his behavior and leadership. Other sources say that Seale left willingly in 1974.

Seale also is the author of several books including *Seize the Time: The Story of the Black Panther Party and Huey P. Newton*; *A Lonely Rage: The Autobiography of Bobby Seale*; *Barbeque'n with Bobby*; and *Power to the People: The World of the Black Panthers*. He has also appeared in several popular films including director Spike Lee's *Malcolm X* and *The Sixties: The Year That Shaped a Generation*. As of this writing, Seale is the last surviving original member of the BPP.

Eldridge Cleaver (1935–1998)

Eldridge Cleaver was born Leroy Eldridge Cleaver in Wabbaseka, Arkansas, a rural, predominately black town on August 31, 1935. During his early childhood, the Cleavers moved to Los Angeles, California, in search of better economic opportunities and a life free from the open racism they experienced in the South. The streets of Watts, Los Angeles, were like a siren song for the young Eldridge. As an older child and teenager, he fell in with the wrong crowds and became a petty thief. In the vain hopes of rehabilitating him, a judge sent Cleaver to a number of reform schools wherein he fell deeper into crime. He served two and a half years in California's Soledad Prison for selling marijuana and was released in 1957. After a series of sexual assaults against white and black women, which he writes about in his best-selling 1968 publication, *Soul on Ice*, Cleaver was imprisoned and convicted again in 1958, this time for assault with the intent to kill and sentenced to imprisonment for two to fourteen years. In prison, he read broadly and became a follower of Malcolm X's black nationalism. He was released in 1966.

During the winter of 1967, Cleaver moved to San Francisco in hopes of joining the Black Power movement and joined with Ed Bullins, Marvin Jackman, and Willie Dale, three black artists, to open the Black House, an arts center focused on black cultural development and artistic expression. By the end of the year, Cleaver was unhappy with Bullins's, Jackman's, and Dale's expressions of African American cultural nationalism and became the minister of information for the BPP. He published sections of *Soul on Ice* with *Ramparts*, a progressive, Catholic magazine.

When *Soul on Ice* was published in 1968, Cleaver became an instant literary celebrity. It became clear that he had been influenced the Frantz Fanon, the theorist and author. Cleaver was also influenced by and compared to his contemporary, James Baldwin, the prolific novelist, essayist, and activist. The book is written primarily for white and black young people who were not as burdened with the racial antipathies of the past and who were prepared to challenge white racism, struggle for racial equality, and do away with their parents' myths. The writer Maxwell Geismar called *Soul on Ice* "a handsome account of those years in the early sixties when the Civil Rights Campaign stirred up the national psyche that had been unnaturally comatose, slothful, and evasive since the McCarthyite trauma."[2]

Cleaver ran for president of the United States with the Peace and Freedom Party in 1968. The Peace and Freedom Party was founded in 1967 in California to oppose racism, sexism, and the war in Vietnam. Such a run for the highest office in the land by a black ex-convict and self-described revolutionary was a publicity stunt at best. Cleaver lost to Richard Nixon, but his run laid the foundation for later electoral bids by Black Panthers, including Bobby Seale's run for the Oakland mayoralty in the early 1970s.

In April 1968, Cleaver became the minister of information for the BPP. In his position, he was the national spokesperson of the group and was expected to use his eloquence and new-found celebrity, two things that Huey P. Newton lacked, for the benefit of the party. Cleaver and Bobby Hutton, the 17-year-old treasurer of the Oakland BPP, were involved in a shoot-out with the Oakland City Police that left Hutton dead and two police officers wounded. Cleaver was arrested and held on $50,000 bail. Rather than risk imprisonment, Cleaver obtained asylum in the Caribbean Island nation of Cuba in late 1968, and subsequently the north African city of Algiers, Algeria, where he and his wife Kathleen Cleaver set up the international section of the BPP. In Algeria, he and his supporters organized a Pan-African cultural festival, bringing together intellectuals and artists from throughout the African diaspora to celebrate black and African culture. Nina Simone, the famed pianist, singer, political activist, and composer, was in attendance as was Stokely Carmichael and the South African singer Miriam Makeba. Cleaver and his compatriots also traveled throughout the Maghreb and Asian nations seeking to shore up allies and secure commitments from like-minded organizations in their fight against colonialism and imperialism.

By the winter of 1971, internal ideological fissures within the party became public. On one side stood Cleaver and the international section who called for armed revolution within the United States. On the other side was Huey P. Newton and the Central Committee who, though not opposed to armed struggle, favored creating and sustaining survival programs. With Bobby Seale entangled in legal battles, Newton possessed almost complete control over the organization and in February 1971 expelled Cleaver and the entire international section of the party. Cleaver lived in France from 1972 to 1975 after receiving asylum there. He returned to the United States in 1975 at which point his charges were reduced and he served time on parole and performing community service.

In the 1980s and 1990s, Cleaver made a political about-face: he rejected all the Black Panthers' tenets including armed revolution and Marxist-Leninism, converted to evangelical Christianity and Mormonism, and embraced the conservative wing of the Republican Party. Cleaver died in 1998 at the age of 62.

Notes

1. Joshua Bloom and Waldo E. Martin, *Black against Empire: The History and Politics of the Black Panther Party* (Berkeley: University of California Press, 2013), 60.
2. Eldridge Cleaver, *Soul on Ice* (New York: Dell Publishing, 1992), 11.

Glossary

Black nationalism: A broad set of political ideas that argue that African Americans constitute a nation within the United States based on their shared experiences with racism, slavery, segregation, and continued oppression.

Brothers from the Block: Gang members, drug dealers, hustlers, pimps, prostitutes, the black lumpenproletariat, whom the Panthers saw as part of the vanguard social and political change.

Colonialism: For the Black Panther Party, "colonialism" was an accurate political term to describe an unbalanced and oppressive economic, cultural, and political relationship wherein African Americans were housed in segregated communities and exploited for the sole purpose of the mother country, in this case, the government of the United States of America.

Lumpenproletariat: Socially and economically marginalized groups of people who worked outside the formal economy. Marxists usually considered this class of people as counterrevolutionary and not capable of being politically organized.

Marxist-Leninism: The political theory adopted by the Black Panther Party based upon the ideas created and promulgated by German philosopher Karl Marx and adapted and applied by Russian theorist Vladimir Lenin. The theory called for the creation of a socialist state.

Mother country radicals: Famous white celebrities and/or white leftist political activists belonging to local, state, and national progressive political organizations that supported the aims and goals of the Black Panther Party.

Pig: Any official of law enforcement, local or federal. Black Panther Party leaders saw agents of the Federal Bureau of Investigation as well as members of state and local law enforcement as members of a system that oppressed and murdered black people.

Second Amendment: A U.S. Constitutional right that states "A well-regulated Militia, being necessary to the security of a free State, the right of the people to keep and bear Arms, shall not be infringed."

Self-defense: The right and ability to resist physical attack and protect one's family and property using physical force.

Self-determination: The right and ability to regulate and govern the social, political, and economic institutions in one's community.

Vamp: The term was often used to suggest a police invasion or raid on a Black Panther Party headquarters or residence as in "the police are vamping on headquarters." Such vamps were usually self-styled, local police incursions using military-style techniques and equipment, which included armed tanks, high-powered weapons, and riot gear to subdue the Panthers and intimidate and obtain community submission and support.

Primary Documents

There are tens of thousands of primary documents written by and about the Black Panther Party (BPP). The primary documents below are organized into three groups: materials written by the Panthers, public speeches given by Panthers, and government documents written about the BPP.

Executive Mandate No. 1: Statement by the Minister of Defense, Delivered May 2, 1967, at Sacramento, California, State Capitol Building

When the BPP was first organized, it was legal for an ordinary citizen to carry a firearm in public spaces in the state of California. Huey P. Newton and Bobby Seale used this fact to start armed police patrols on the streets of Oakland. It was not the first time African Americans banded together with weapons in hopes of protecting their community from outside violence. In the 20th century throughout America, Southern African Americans sometimes formed gun clubs to ward off rampaging white vigilante groups. However, the formation of the BPP marked the first time that African Americans created a nationwide organization that openly subscribed to armed self-defense. By openly calling for armed self-defense and dramatic changes in U.S. politics, the Panthers were perceived to be a threat to the nation. The Panthers openly opposed attempts to disarm them in California, but they eventually had their Second Amendment rights curtailed by the California state government when the Mulford Act passed.

The Black Panther Party for Self Defense calls upon the American people in general and Black people in particular to take careful note of the racist California Legislature which is now considering legislation aimed to keep the Black people disarmed and powerless at the very same time that racist police agencies throughout the country are intensifying the terror, brutality, murder, and repression of Black people.

At the same time that the American government is waging a racist war of genocide in Vietnam, the concentration camps in which Japanese Americans were interned during World War II are being renovated and expanded. Since America has historically reserved the most barbaric treatment for non-white people, we are forced to conclude that these concentration camps are being prepared for Black people who are determined to gain their freedom by any means necessary. The enslavement of Black people from the very beginning of this country, the genocide practiced on the American Indians and the confining of the survivors on reservations, the lynching of thousands of Black men and women, the dropping of atomic bombs on Hiroshima and Nagasaki, and now the cowardly massacre in Vietnam, all testify to the fact that towards people of color the racist power structure of American has but one policy: repression, genocide, terror, and the big stick.

Black people have begged, prayed, petitioned, demonstrated, and everything else to get the racist power structure of America to right the wrongs which have historically been perpetrated against black people. All of these efforts have been answered by more repression, deceit, and hypocrisy. As the aggression of the racist American government escalates in Vietnam, the police agencies of America escalate the repression of Black people throughout the ghettos of America. Vicious police dogs, cattle prods and increased patrols have become familiar sights in black communities. City Hall turns a deaf ear to the pleas of Black people for relief from this increasing terror.

The Black Panther Party for Self Defense believes that the time has come for Black people to arm themselves against this terror before it is too late. The pending Mulford Act brings the hour of doom one step nearer. A people who have suffered so much for so long at the hands of a racist society, must draw the line somewhere. We believe that the Black communities of America must rise up as one man to halt the progression of a trend that leads inevitably to their total destruction.

Source: United States Congress, Senate, Committee on Government Operations, Permanent Subcommittee on Investigations. Riots, Civil and Criminal Disorders: Hearings before the Permanent Subcommittee on Investigations on the Committee on Government Operations, the United States Senate. Washington: U.S. GPO 1967. https://babel.hathitrust.org/cgi/pt?id=mdp.39076006970151;view=1up; seq=33. Accessed: January 13, 2017.

Huey P. Newton, Executive Mandate No. 2, June 29, 1967

The Student Nonviolent Coordinating Committee (SNCC) was one of the most important African American civil rights organizations in the 1960s. Comprised primarily of black college students, it was committed to opposing structural racism. In the late 1960s, SNCC was influenced by the expanding Black Power movement and hoped to expand its influence in northern, midwestern, and western cities. As a young organization dedicated to challenging police violence, the BPP wanted to extend its influence throughout the South. After extensive discussion and maneuvers, SNCC members joined the party. Stokely Carmichael, the former chairman of SNCC who would later be known as Kwame Ture an advocate of Pan-Africanism, became a field marshal in the organization.

So Let This Be Heard. . .

Brother Stokely Carmichael:

Because you have distinguished yourself in the struggle for the total liberation of Black people from oppression in racist white America;

Because you have acted courageously and show great fortitude under the most adverse circumstances;

Because you have proven yourself a true revolutionary guided by a great feeling of love for our people;

Because you have set such a fine example, in the tradition of Brother Malcolm, or dedicating your entire life to the struggle of

Black Liberation, inspiring our youth and providing a model for others to emulate;

Because you have refused to serve in the oppressor's racist mercenary, aggressive war machine, showing that you know who your true friends and enemies are;

Because of your new endeavor to organize and liberate the Crown Colony of Washington, D.C, you will inevitably be forced to confront, deal with, and conquer the racist Washington Police Department which functions as the protector of the racist dog power structure, occupying the Black Community in the same manner and for the same reasons that the U.S. Armed forces occupy South Vietnam;

You are hereby drafted into the Black Panther Party for Self Defense, invested with the rank of Field Marshal delegated the following authority, power, and responsibility:

To establish revolutionary law, order and justice in the territory lying between the Continental Divide East to the Atlantic Ocean, North of the Mason-Dixon Line to the Canadian Border, South of the Mason-Dixon Line to the Gulf of Mexico.

So Let it Be Done.

Source: United States Congress, Senate, Committee on Government Operations, Permanent Subcommittee on Investigations. Riots, Civil and Criminal Disorders: Hearings before the Permanent Subcommittee on Investigations on the Committee on Government Operations, the United States Senate. Washington: U.S. GPO 1967. https://babel.hathitrust.org/cgi/pt?id=mdp.39076006970151;view=1up; seq=33. Accessed: January 13, 2017.

Huey P. Newton, Executive Mandate No. 3, March 1, 1968

In late 1967 and early 1968, party chapters around the nation were increasingly involved in violent altercations with local and state police departments and rival political organizations. Sometimes these altercations were instigated by the police and sometimes by the young revolutionaries themselves. On numerous occasions, party offices were raided by police. It was common for police to enter Panther members' homes in hopes of making arrests oftentimes without an arrest warrant in clear violation of Panthers' constitutional rights. In response to growing police repression, Huey P. Newton, the minister of self-defense, issued his third executive mandate.

So let it be heard:

Because of the St. Valentine's Day massacre of February 14, 1929, in which outlaws donned the uniforms of Policemen, posed as such, and thereby gained entrance to locked doors controlled by rival outlaws with whom they were contending for control of the bootlegging industry in Chicago, and because these gangsters, gaining entry through their disguise as Policemen, proceed to exterminate their rivals with machinegun fire, we believe that prudence would dictate that one should be alert when opening one's door to strangers, late at night in the wee hours of the morning—even when these strangers wear the uniform of policemen. History teaches us that the man in the uniform may or may not be a policeman authorized to enter the homes of the people; and

Taking notice of the fact that (1) on January 16, 1968, at 3:30 A.M., members of the San Francisco Police Department kicked down the door and made an illegal entry, and searched of the home of Eldridge Cleaver, Minister of Information. These Pigs had no search warrant, no arrest warrant, and were therefore not authorized to enter. They were not invited in. Permission for them to enter was explicitly denied by the Minister of Information. Present was Sister Kathleen Cleaver, our Communications Secretary and wife to our Minister of Information, and Brother Emory Douglas, our Revolutionary Artist.

Taking further notice of the fact that (2) on February 25, 1968, several uniformed gestapos of the Berkeley Pig Department, accompanied by several other white men in plainclothes, bearing an assortment of shotguns, rifles, and service revolvers, made a forceful, unlawful entry and search of the home of Bobby Seale, Chairman of our Party, and his wife, Sister Artie Seale. These Pigs had no warrant to search or to arrest. When asked by Chairman Bobby to produce a warrant, they arrogantly stated that they did not need one. They had no authority to enter—what they did have was the power of the gun. Thus, we are confronted with a critical situation. Our organization has received serious threats from certain racist elements of White America, including the Oakland, Berkeley, and San Francisco Pig Departments. Threats to take our lives, to exterminate us. We cannot determine when any of these elements, or a combination of them, may move to implement these threats. We must be alert to the danger at all times. We will not fall victim to a St. Valentine's Massacre. Therefore, those who approach our doors in the manner of outlaws, who seek to enter homes illegally, unlawfully and in a rowdy fashion, those who kick our doors down with no authority and seek to ransack our homes in violation of our HUMAN RIGHTS, will henceforth be treated as outlaws, as gangsters, as evildoers. We have no way of determining that a man in a uniform involved in a forced outlaw entry into our home is in fact a Guardian of the Law. He is acting like a lawbreaker and we must make an appropriate response.

We draw the line at the threshold of our doors. It is therefore mandated as a general order to all members of the Black Panther Party for Self Defense that all members must acquire the technical equipment to defend their homes and their dependents and shall do so. Any member of the Party having such technical equipment and fails to defend his threshold shall be expelled from the Party for Life.

So let this be done.

Source: United States Congress, Senate, Committee on Government Operations, Permanent Subcommittee on Investigations. Riots, Civil and Criminal Disorders: Hearings before the Permanent Subcommittee on Investigations on the Committee on Government Operations, the United States Senate. Washington: U.S. GPO 1967. https://babel.hathitrust.org/cgi/pt?id=mdp.39076006970151;view=1up; seq=33. Accessed: January 23, 2017.

Legal First Aid, 1970

The BPP conducted a variety of the programs to help indigent black people in cities. An important one was the Legal Aid for Prisoners Program. It was "maintained primarily through correspondence with prisoners—the sending and receiving of information needed to handle prisoners' legal matters and affairs." The New Haven BPP chapter expand upon the legal aid program to create the Legal First Aid Program, one of the chapter's most far-reaching programs. One of the mainstays of white liberalism was that local police treated citizens equally and did not harass or exploit African Americans. The Legal First Aid Program flier, included in the People's News Service and expounded upon in the Panthers' legal clinic, provided basic legal advice for New Haven's African American residents about how to handle an encounter with the police. The flier informed them to memorize and assert 12 of their most basic rights and react in appropriate ways during confrontation with local police.

This pocket lawyer is provided as a means of keeping the people up to date on their rights. We are always the first to be arrested while the fascist police officers are constantly trying to pretend that rights are extended equally to all people. Carry it with you.

1. If you are stopped and/or arrested by the police, you may remain silent; you do not have to answer questions about alleged crimes; you should provide your name and address only if requested (although it is not absolutely clear that you must do so). But then do so, and at all times remember the Fifth Amendment.

2. If a police officer is not in uniform, ask him to show his identification. He has no authority over you unless he properly identifies himself. Beware of persons posing as police officers.

3. Police have no right to search your car or your home unless they have a search warrant, probable cause, or your consent. They may conduct no exploratory search, that is, one for evidence of a crime unconnected with the one you are being questioned about. (Thus, a stop for an auto violation does not give the rights to search the auto). You are not required to consent to search, therefore, you should not consent. IN FRONT OF WITNESSES IF POSSIBLE. If you do not consent, the police will have the burden in court of showing probable cause. Arrest may be corrected later.

4. You may NOT RESIST ARREST FORCIBLY OR BY GOING LIMP, even if you are innocent. To do so is a separate crime of which you can be convicted if you are acquitted for the original charge. DO NOT RESIST ARREST UNDER ANY CIRCUMSTANCES.

5. If you are stopped and/or arrested the police may search you by patting you on the outside of your clothing. You can be stripped of your personal possessions. Do not carry anything that includes the name of your employer or friends.

6. Do not engage in "friendly" conversation with the officers on the way to the or at the station. Once you are arrested, there is little likelihood that anything you say will get you released.

7. As soon as you have been booked, you have the right to complete at least two phone calls—one to a relative, friend, or attorney; the other to a bail bondsman. If you can, call the Black Panther Party . . .and the Party will post bail if possible.

8. You must be allowed to hire and see an attorney immediately.

9. You do not have to give any statement to the police, nor do you have to sign any statement you might give them; and, therefore, you should

not sign anything. Take the fifth and the Fourteenth Amendments, because you cannot be forced to testify against yourself.

10. You must be allowed to post bail in most cases, but you must be able to pay the bail bondsman's fee. If you cannot pay the fee, you ask the judge to release you from custody without bail or to lower your bail. But he does not have to do so.

11. The police must bring you into the court or release you within 48 hours after your arrest (unless time ends on a week-end or holiday, and then they must bring you before a judge the first day court is in session).

12. If you do not have money to hire an attorney, IMMEDIATELY ASK THE POLICE TO GET YOU AN ATTORNEY WITHOUT CHARGE.

Source: Black Panther Party of Connecticut, Legal Aid Flier, John R. Williams Papers, Box 3, Folder 23, MS1398. Manuscripts and Archives, Yale University Library.

Telephone Interview with Bobby Seale, Radio Havana, August 13, 1968

In the 1960s, the U.S. Central Intelligence Agency (CIA) supported the Foreign Broadcast Information Service (FBIS) whose primary goal was "to monitor and process foreign broadcasts for the benefit of all government agencies needing the service." To that end, the FBIS monitored and transcribed various interviews with Black Panther leaders and rank-and-file members who traveled abroad and spoke with reporters. Below is an interview that BPP chairman Bobby Seale conducted on Radio Havana, a station in Cuba.

Question. What can you tell us about the trial of Huey Newton in Oakland, California, and about the Black Panther Party's activities to obtain the release of its Minister of Defense?

Answer. The members of the Black Panther Party and, in general the U.S. Negro community, see that so-called trial as a form of legalized lynching. They see it in this manner because of the legalistic maneuver against Huey Newton is nothing more than the continuation of the repeatedly aggressive policy of the racist, capitalist, and imperialist structure of white power in the United States against the Negro population of this country.

The U.S. Negro community has entered the stage of open rebellion all over the country and it is doing it with weapons in hand, confronting the racist police, the pigs in uniform who have invaded our communities as if they were foreign occupation forces. In Seattle, Washington, where the Black Panther Party is already organized, two policemen were killed and nine wounded in a recent clash with the Negro population and members of the Black Panther Party. In New York, four members of the party were arrested and two policemen were shot and killed with shotgun fire at close range by other members of the Black Panther Party. In Los Angeles, three party members were assassinated by the racist policemen occupying that city's Negro community. And Thursday night, seven other members were arrested by racist pigs of the local police.

In other cities, the Negro community has received our message that the only way to successfully face the exploitation and abuses of the white power racist structure and of the policemen at its service is the organized use of weapons and force. Huey P. Newton, our Defense Minister, must be released immediately. If this does not happen, white power will be provoking and will have to face the Negro population in a civil war on a national scale.

Question. What can you tell us, Bobby Seale, about the third anniversary of the rebellion of the Negro ghetto of Watts in Los Angeles, California, which will be marked on 18 August, and about the tricontinental call to hold a worldwide day of solidarity with the struggle of the U.S. Negro people?

Answer. The Negro rebellion, which began 3 or 4 years ago, has grown tenfold. Since the July 18, 1964 riot in Harlem and those in Watts a year later, and after Newark and Detroit, over 250 Negro rebellions have taken place in the United States, according to our estimates. The Negro population now understands that our struggle must graduate to a higher stage, that we should use Molotov cocktails and stones, employing tactics in which small groups of three or four men work with any type of weapons and explosives. In short, with anything we can lay our hands on to expel the racist pigs from our communities and take control of our territory and begin to work toward a social state, a socialist state, a socialist system in those areas, a system which will immediately put an end to racism in this country.

We see all the Negro rebellions such as Watts and all the revolutionary struggles within the United States—with the Black Panther Party in the vanguard—as a great liberation movement of the Negro population, as a great movement joined with the movements for peace and freedom and other white groups who advocate revolution to destroy the imperialist and racist structure which exists in this country. As for the day of solidarity which is to take place on 18 August, we definitely support it.

Question. As for coordination with other organizations such as SNCC, what can you tell us?

Answer. Well, the Black Panther Party has developed as a vanguard organization and at the present has moved to the front of the struggle, and we expect the support of everybody.

Question. Have you had contacts with student organizations in this stage of the struggle?

Answer. Yes, we have made contacts with many organizations and many students have joined the Party to fight within its ranks, because they student program is included in the growth of our organization.

Source: https://www.cia.gov/library/center-for-the-study-of-intelligence/csi -publications/books-and-monographs/foreign-broadcast-information-service. United States Congress, Senate, Committee on Government Operations, Permanent Subcommittee on Investigations. Riots, Civil and Criminal Disorders: Hearings before the Permanent Subcommittee on Investigations on the Committee on Government Operations, the United States Senate. Washington: U.S. GPO 1967. https:// babel.hathitrust.org/cgi/pt?id=mdp.39076006970151;view=1up;seq=33. Accessed: January 13, 2017.

Excerpt, August 1968, Radio Address Given by George Mason
Murray, Minister of Education, during a Trip to Havana, Cuba

*The Black Panthers saw the Cuban people as allies in the struggle against
American racism. In fact, several party members sought refuge in the island
nation, including Huey P. Newton and Assata Shakur. George Mason
Murray visited the nation in hopes of securing Cuban support for the
BPP and internationalizing the Panthers' cause. Huey P. Newton and
Bobby Seale often spoke of how the organization was focused on recruiting
the lumpenproletariat, black men and women who were socially and economically marginalized. That Murray, a professor at San Francisco State
College, was affiliated with the Panthers demonstrates the organization's
appeal to college-educated, middle-class African Americans, who served
critical roles locally an internationally.*

Brothers and Sisters, we must be aware of the imperialist dogs. We
must understand the imperialists murdered Martin Luther King and
murdered Malcolm X, that they will definitely murder any of us.
Now with this understanding, what we must do is to collect our arms.
To arm ourselves with guns and force in an organized manner to resist
racists' oppression . . .
    Black people of America, we must not allow the imperialists to kill
Huey P. Newton. They think that if they kill Huey Newton, that they
will be putting an end to guerrilla warfare. What do we mean by guerrilla warfare? We mean to organize the black people in two's and
three's and four's and five's to assassinate the police who kill us. When
we speak of guerrilla warfare, we mean the opening of schools for black
people throughout the United States where we can be taught our true
cause and our true history and our true way of life. When we speak of
guerrilla warfare, we mean the opening of hospitals in the black community where more black people can be born without dying from
being born at home, or without dying from malnutrition or without
dying from starvation. And when we speak of guerrilla warfare, we
mean the opening up of farms for black people where black youths
can be trained, where black people can produce their own food, where
black people in the United States can live in peace. And when we
speak of guerrilla warfare, we mean sending black men in the

United States to resist racism in their homes, rather than being sent 10,000 miles away to die fighting the Vietnamese who have never called us nigger . . .

We know that the imperialist dogs in the United States will attempt to arrest us—maybe even kill us—for coming here and spreading our truth to our Asian, African, and Latin American brothers, but we want you to know this: If we die tonight, we can be like Martin Luther King: we've been to the mountain top, we've seen the promised land, we've seen the truth of struggle. And we would like to say to black people, ever onward to victory. We know that we will be free, we know that we shall overcome, and as our brothers say in Spanish, "venceremos."

Source: United States Congress, Senate, Committee on Government Operations, Permanent Subcommittee on Investigations. Riots, Civil and Criminal Disorders: Hearings before the Permanent Subcommittee on Investigations on the Committee on Government Operations, the United States Senate. Washington: U.S. GPO 1967. https://babel.hathitrust.org/cgi/pt?id=mdp.39076006970151;view=1up; seq=41. Accessed December 30, 2016.

Federal Bureau of Investigation Plans to Eliminate the Progressive African American Organizations

FBI informants infiltrated the Black Panther Party in cities throughout the nation. By inserting informants and inciting agents into chapters, branches, and affiliates; disseminating misinformation about local and national BPP leaders; creating and spreading imaginative counterintelligence programs; and creating and exacerbating tensions within the organization and between the Panthers and other organizations, the FBI stunted the growth of the party, and was, at least partially, responsible for destroying it. Below are communications from the national director of the FBI to Special Agents in Charge of counterintelligence in towns and cities throughout the nation discussing ways to deal with black nationalist organizations in general and the BPP specifically.

Airtel to Special Agent in Charge, Albany et al., from Director Federal Bureau of Investigation, August 25, 1967

Offices receiving copies of this letter are instructed to immediately establish a control file, captioned as above, and to assign responsibility for following and coordinating this new counterintelligence program to an experienced and imaginative Special Agent well versed in investigations relating to black nationalist, hate-type organizations. The field office control file used under this program may be maintained in a pending inactive status until such time as specific operation or technique is placed under consideration for implementation.

The purpose of this new counterintelligence endeavor is to expose, disrupt, misdirect, discredit, or otherwise neutralize the activities of black nationalist, hate-type organizations and groupings, their leadership, spokesmen, membership, and supporters, and to counter their propensity for violence and civil disorder. The activities of all such groups of intelligence are of interest to this Bureau and must be followed on a continuous basis so we will be in a position to promptly take advantage of all opportunities for counterintelligence and to inspire action in instances where circumstances warrant. The pernicious background of such groups, their duplicity, and devious maneuvers must be exposed to public scrutiny where such publicity will have a neutralizing effect. Efforts of the various groups to consolidate their forces or to recruit new or youthful adherents must be frustrated. No opportunity should be missed to exploit through counterintelligence techniques the organizational and personal conflicts of the leaderships of the groups and where possible an effort should be made to capitalize upon existing conflicts between competing black nationalist organizations. When an opportunity is apparent to disrupt or neutralize black nationalist, hate-type organizations through the cooperation of established local news media or through such contact with sources available to the Seat of Government, in every instance careful attention must be given to the proposal to insure the targeted group is disrupted, ridiculed, or discredited through the publicity and not merely publicized. Consideration should be given to techniques to preclude violence-prone or rabble rouser leaders of hate groups from spreading their philosophy publicly or through various mass communication media.

Many individuals currently active in black nationalist organizations have backgrounds of immorality, subversive activity, and criminal records. Through your investigations of key agitators, you should endeavor to establish their unsavory backgrounds. Be alert to determine evidence of misappropriation of funds or other types of personal conduct on the part of militant nationalist leaders so any practical or warranted counterintelligence may be instituted.

Intensified attention under this program should be afforded to the activities of such groups as the Student Nonviolent Coordinating Committee, the Southern Christian Leadership Committee, Revolutionary Action Movement, the Deacons for Self Defense and Justice, Congress of Racial Equality, and the Nation of Islam. Particular emphasis should be given to extremists who direct the activities and policies of revolutionary or militant group such as Stokely Carmichael, H. Rap Brown, Elijah Muhammad, and Maxwell Stanford.

At this time the Bureau is setting up no requirement for status letters to be periodically submitted under this program. It will be incumbent upon you to insure the program is being afforded necessary and continuing attention and that no opportunities will be overlooked for counterintelligence.

This program should not be confused with the program entitled "Communist Party, USA, Counterintelligence Program, Internal Security—C," (Bufile 100-3-104), which is directed against the Communist Party and related organizations or the program entitled "Counterintelligence Program, Internal Security, Disruption of Hate Groups" (Bufile 157-9), which is directed against Klan and hate-type groups primarily consisting of white memberships.

All Special Agents personnel responsible for the investigation of black nationalist, hate-type organizations and their memberships should be alerted to our counterintelligence interest and each investigative Agent has a responsibility to call to the attention of the counterintelligence coordinator suggestions and possibilities for implementing the program. You are also cautioned that the nature of this new endeavor is such that under no circumstances should the existence of the program be made known outside the Bureau and appropriate within-office security should be afforded to sensitive operations and techniques considered under the programs.

No counterintelligence action under this program may be initiated by the field without specific prior Bureau authorization.

You are urged to take an enthusiastic and imaginative approach to this new counterintelligence endeavor and the Bureau will be pleased to entertain any suggestions or techniques you may recommend.

Source: Records of the Federal Bureau of Investigation, 1868–2008, Classification 157, Civil Unrest, Case Files, 1957–1978, Charlotte, North Carolina, 157-6109-1. https://catalog. archives.gov/id 5562909. Accessed: January 2, 2017.

Airtel to Special Agent in Charge, Albany et al., from Director Federal Bureau of Investigation, March 4, 1968

By letter dated 8/25/67 the following offices were advised of the beginning of a Counterintelligence Program against militant Black Nationalist-Hate Groups:

Albany	Memphis
Atlanta	Newark
Baltimore	New Orleans
Boston	New York
Buffalo	Philadelphia
Charlotte	Phoenix
Chicago	Pittsburgh
Cincinnati	Richmond
Cleveland	St. Louis
Detroit	San Francisco
Jackson	Washington Field
Los Angeles	

Each of the above offices was to designate a Special Agent to coordinate this program. Replies to this letter indicated an interest in counterintelligence against militant black national groups that foment violence and several offices outlined procedures which had been effective in the past. For example, Washington Field Office had furnished information about a new Nation of Islam grade school to appropriate authorities in the District of Columbia who investigated to determine if the school conformed to District regulation for private schools. In the process WFO obtained background information on the parents of each pupil.

The Revolutionary Action Movement (RAM), a pro-Chinese communist group, was active in Philadelphia, Pa., in the summer of 1967. The Philadelphia Office alerted local police, who then put RAM leaders under close scrutiny. They were arrested on every possible charge until they could no longer make bail. As a result, RAM leaders spent most of the summer in jail and no violence traceable to RAM took place.

The Counterintelligence Program is now being expanded to include 41 offices. Each of the offices in this program should designate an Agent familiar with black nationalist activity, and interested in counterintelligence to coordinate this program. This Agent will be responsible for the periodic progress letters being requested, but each Agent working this type of case should participate in the formulation of counterintelligence operations.

<u>Goals</u>
For maximum effectiveness of the Counterintelligence Program, and to prevent wasted effort, long-range goals are being set.

1. Prevent the coalition of militant black nationalist groups. In unity there is strength; a truism that is no less valid for all its triteness. An effective coalition of black nationalist groups might be the first step toward a real "Mau Mau" in America, the beginning of a true black revolution.

2. Prevent the rise of a "messiah" who could unify, and electrify, the militant nationalist movement. Malcolm X might have been such a "Messiah"; he is the martyr of the movement today. Martin Luther King, Stokely Carmichael, and Elijah Muhammad all aspire to this position. Elijah Muhammad is less of a threat because of his age. King could be a very real contender for this position should he abandon his supposed "obedience" to "white, liberal doctrines" (nonviolence) and embrace black nationalism. Carmichael has the necessary charisma to be a real threat in this way.

3. Prevent violence on the part of black nationalist groups. This is of primary importance, and is, of course, a goal of our investigative activity; it should also be a goal of the Counterintelligence Program. Through counterintelligence it should be possible to pinpoint potential troublemakers and neutralize them before they exercise their potential for violence.

4. Prevent militant black nationalist groups and leaders from gaining respectability, by discrediting them to three separate segments of the community. The goal of discrediting black nationalists must be handled tactically in three ways. You must discredit these groups and individuals to, first, the responsible Negro community. Second, they must be discredited to the white community, both the responsible community and to "liberals" who have vestiges of sympathy for militant black nationalist simply because they are Negroes. Third, these groups must be discredited in the eyes of Negro radicals, the followers of the

movement. This last area requires entirely different tactics from the first two. Publicity about violent tendencies and radical statements merely enhance black nationalists to the last group; it adds "respectability" in a different way

5. A final goal should be to prevent long-range growth of militant black nationalist organizations, especially among youth. Specific tactics to prevent these groups from converting young people must be developed.

Besides these five goals counterintelligence is a valuable part of our regular investigative program as it often produces positive information.

Source: Records of the Federal Bureau of Investigation, 1868–2008, Classification 157, Civil Unrest, Case Files, 1957–1978, Alexandria, Virginia, 157-48-1. https://catalog. archives.gov/id/5060504. Accessed: January 24, 2017.

Memo to Special Agent in Charge, San Francisco, from Director, Federal Bureau of Investigation, September 30, 1968

In view of the continued increase of violent activities on the part of the Black Panther Party (BPP), it is mandatory that the counterintelligence program against this Party be accelerated. Each division receiving this letter either has an active BPP chapter in its division or according to information received the BPP is either forming or attempting to form a chapter in that division.

By 10/14/68 each division must submit concrete suggestions as to proposed counterintelligences activity to be taken against the BPP in its particular division as well as suggestions as to what action can be taken against the BPP on a national level. In keeping with Bureau policy, no policy should be taken on these proposals without prior Bureau authority.

In line with the above, consideration should be given as to how factionalism can be created between local leaders as well as national leaders and how BPP organizational efforts can be neutralized. Given consideration to action which will create suspicion among the leaders with respect to their financial sources, suspicion concerning their respective spouses, suspicion as to who may be cooperating with law enforcement and suspicion as to who may be attempting to gain complete control of the organization for his own private betterment. In addition, consideration should be given to the best method of exploiting foreign visits BPP members have made as well as the best method of creating opposition to this Party on part of the majority of the residents of the ghetto area.

This matter must be given continued attention and your imagination and resourcefulness must be employed for the Bureau to be successful in this most serious matter.

Source: Records of the Federal Bureau of Investigation, 1868–2008, Classification 157, Civil Unrest, Case Files, 1957–1978, Baltimore, Maryland 157-2520-1. https:// catalog. archives.gov/id/5215226. Accessed: January 24, 2017.

Jean and Larry Powell, Excerpt of Testimony before the Permanent Subcommittee on Investigations, June 1969

Larry Clayton Powell was a member of the BPP in Los Angeles, California. He eventually rose through the ranks to become a captain and a member of the Black Guard, an armed body within the BPP, before he was expelled. Jean Powell was secretary with the Black Panthers in Los Angeles and eventually became a national secretary at the Black Panther headquarters in Oakland, California, before she was expelled. They were both subpoenaed to appear before the U.S. Senate for a subcommittee hearing. The Powells delivered prepared statements to the subcommittee and answered a litany of questions from Senator John L. McClellan of Arkansas (the chairman), Senator Karl Mundt of South Dakota, Senator Abraham Ribicoff of Connecticut, and Senator Robert Griffin of Michigan. The two testified for hours, offered praise and criticism of the national leadership of the party, and revealed intraparty conflicts, tensions, and rivalries.

Senator Ribicoff. Would you say of all the organizations operating in the black community, that the Black Panthers are the most active?

Mr. Powell. Yes.

Mrs. Powell. Yes, I would say so

Senator Ribicoff. They are the most active?

Mrs. Powell. Yes.

Senator Ribicoff. And in many of the black communities there is a general fear?

Mr. Powell. Of the Black Panther Party?

Senator Ribicoff. Yes.

Mr. Powell. No.

Senator Ribicoff. There is no fear of the Black Panther Party?

Mr. Powell. No.

Mrs. Powell. There is respect.

Senator Ribicoff. And yet in the black community, the individuals don't want to cross the Black Panthers, individually or as a group, isn't that correct?

Mr. Powell. More or less, yes. But I wouldn't say there was fear of the Black Panther Party.

Senator Ribicoff. The Black Panthers have started around the Nation programs to feed schoolchildren who are hungry before they go to school, isn't that right?

Mr. Powell. Yes.

Mrs. Powell. Yes.

Senator Ribicoff. The children that they feed are not necessarily of Black Panther members. They feed children in the general community, is that correct?

Mr. Powell. Yes.

Senator Ribicoff. The truth is that many of these children are hungry. They go to school without breakfast.

Mrs. Powell. Yes.

Senator Ribicoff. And the Black Panthers are the ones that give them food.

Mr. Powell. Right. But more or less the people of the community give them food because the Black Panther Party hasn't paid a dime for the food. That has been solicited.

Mrs. Powell. Donated.

Senator Ribicoff. The food has been donated, but the Black Panthers are the ones who organize the collecting of food?

Mrs. Powell. Ex-members of the Black Panthers.

Senator Ribicoff. Ex-members?

Mrs. Powell. Ex-members, right.

Senator Ribicoff. Why is it that the Black Panthers are the ones that get credit for feeding the children?

Mr. Powell. Because they are the ones that set the program up.

Senator Ribicoff. They set the program up?

Mr. Powell. Yes.

Mrs. Powell. You see, it took a turn about November or December of 1968. Like people who were in jail, people who were deceased, all this type of thing; these are the people that began to start trying to form different things to help the community.

After all, this mess that went down, then the Black Panthers took credit for it, when really it was half of the people now either in jail, dead, or exiled. They set it up where people from the community donated food, and the children came into these churches to have breakfast.

Senator Ribicoff. But you say that the Black Panther themselves as an organization are not running these feeding programs?

Mr. Powell. They are running them.

Senator Ribicoff. They are running them?

Mr. Powell. Yes.

Mrs. Powell. The Panther Party.

Senator Ribicoff. So the Panther Party is getting credit in the black community and white community of feeding children who are hungry?

Mr. Powell. Right.

Senator Ribicoff. To this extent, the overall white or black society are pretty stupid in not feeding hungry children and let the Black Panthers get credit for doing something worthwhile in feeding children?

Mr. Powell. I wouldn't say that. I would just say that the Panther Party came to the idea first.

Senator Ribicoff. The Black Panther Party came to the idea first?

Mr. Powell. Yes.

Senator Ribicoff. In other words, all these years the white community didn't see the necessity of feeding hungry children.

Mr. Powell. Evidently, they didn't.

Senator Ribicoff. There is nothing to stop the black community and white community from feeding children now, is there?

Mr. Powell. This is the whole idea.

Senator Ribicoff. As part of feeding the children, there is an educational program in which the children are being inculcated with Black Panther philosophy.

Mr. Powell. This is the idea of feeding the children.

Senator Ribicoff. You feed the children and with the food you are giving them you are talking Black Panther philosophy?

Mr. Powell. This is your key to indoctrinate them.

Senator Ribicoff. And the only contact the black children have with something positive being done for them is—

Mr. Powell. (continuing). Is they got a full stomach.

I would say the only contact the have with something positive is that they are getting a meal.

Senator Ribicoff. In other words, a person with an empty belly getting some food is a pretty positive thing, is it not?

Mr. Powell. Yes, I would say this.

Mrs. Powell. There is something I have to say. This is one thing you must realize. Like you are saying the Black Panther Party, but we can't really say the Black Panther Party because the Party has been destroyed. I mean, the people who really took this and tried to make it something to help people, like I said are either killed or in jail, or expelled from the party.

The people who set up the children's breakfasts meant it to be something good. But like they have this Bunchy Carter Memorial Fund. Bunchy Carter was something that was beautiful in Los Angeles, yet the leadership in Berkeley was talking about getting rid of him and couldn't stand a lot of the things that he was doing.

As soon as he was assassinated, then they come up with this big Bunchy Carter Memorial Fund. That is only bringing in more money for them, and they were getting ready to get rid of him.

The Chairman. You know that, but the general public doesn't know that.

Mrs. Powell. Right.

The Chairman. I saw a television program on national television the other day which showed the Black Panthers feeding children and inculcating the children with revolutionary doctrine, talking about revolution, take to the gun and shoot down the white man.

But this was in connection with a breakfast feeding of children by Black Panthers.

Mrs. Powell. Of course this is going to come in, because they are constantly trying to go on this thing of Huey P. Newton, in which the word "pig" didn't even come in with Huey P. Newton. That came in when the trials began of Huey P. Newton.

Senator Ribicoff. Do you think the Black Panther Party has influence in the black community today?

Mr. Powell. Definitely, yes.

Senator Ribicoff. It definitely has influence?

Mr. Powell. Right.

Source: United States Congress, Senate, Committee on Government Operations, Permanent Subcommittee on Investigations. Riots, Civil and Criminal Disorders: Hearings before the Permanent Subcommittee on Investigations on the Committee on Government Operations, the United States Senate. Washington: U.S. GPO 1967. https://babel.hathitrust.org/cgi/pt?id=mdp.39076006970151;view=1up; seq=41. Accessed: January 17, 2017.

Informant Report, List of People at New Haven Headquarters, Security of Headquarters, January 9, 1970, Dictated to Agent Linda Christianson, Received by Special Agent John A. Danaher, Jr., New Haven, Connecticut

In cities throughout the country, informants strategically and stealthily joined the BPP, attended meetings, and reported their findings to agents in the FBI. Sometimes the information provided offered opportunities to raid or disrupt a chapter or branch and arrest party members. In at least one instance, in Chicago, Illinois, when Fred Hampton was killed by police while he slept, an informant's information was used to kill a Panther member. Often, as is the case with the report below, informants reported the subject of a meeting and provided names of individuals who attended meetings in hopes of offering other surveillance opportunities.

On 1/8/70, at 35 Sylvan Avenue, the following people were present, and it would appear that they are pretty permanent:

> Dolores Burney (y)
> Gloria (Negro) (y)
> Tom (White) (y) Married
> Annie (White) (y)
> Sue (White) (y)
> Cornell Wright (y)
> Diane (s)
> Doug Fauntleroy (s) Married
> Gregory (s)
> Verna Hampton (s) Married
> Bruce Ryles (s)
> Jim Wilson (White) (s)
> "Cheeter" (s) new person
> D. Miranda (s)

Pat Miller (RC)
Vernon Miller (RC) Married
James Ellison (RC)
William Weaver (Hartford)
"Teddy Bear" (Stamford)
Cappy (s)
Y means York Street
S means Sylvan Avenue
RC means Rock Creek
Cappy and Tom are supposed to have gone to the West Coast, the means of travel is not known.

Joel Brown is now in Boston on transfer.

Miranda announced that security on Sylvan Avenue has to begin and the first things to be done involve placing chicken wire over the windows to protect the tear gas shells. Plywood will then be nailed to the door facings. Heavy wood will be crisscrossed over the downstairs front doors.

Snake says he expects to get at least $1000 from a girl name Emma of the Young Patriots.

Miranda wants Weaver and Ryles to make circuit of state placing papers in stores, but they are to concentrate in Waterbury and New Britain at this time, then move to Springfield, Mass.

He said 4,000 copies of the paper are now going to be received in Connecticut each week.

He also stated that Claude Artis seems to want to break from the panthers and form his own militant group in Hartford.

Source: https://catalog.archives.gov/id/5361942. Accessed: January 2, 2017.

Airtel to Special Agent in Charge, Albany et al., from Director Federal Bureau of Investigation, February 10, 1971

Increasing evidence points to rising dissension within the BPP causing serious morale problems and strained relationships among Panther hierarchy. Primary causes of these internal problems appears to be dictatorial, irrational, and capricious conduct of Huey P. Newton. His extreme sensitivity to any criticism, jealousness of other leaders, and belief he is some form of deity are causing severe problems within the group. Newton's relationship with Cleaver and other top leaders is strained. He has recently expelled or disciplined several dedicated Panthers including Elbert Howard, Deputy Minister of Information; Connie Matthews, International Representative and Newton's secretary; Elmer Pratt and companions who were involved in the BPP underground and operation . . . and the "New York 21" who were a leading cause celebre of Pantherism.

This dissension coupled with financial difficulties offers an exceptional opportunity to further disrupt, aggravate, and possibly neutralize this organization with counterintelligence. In light of above developments, this program has been intensified by selected offices and should be further expanded to increase measurably the pressure on the BPP and its leaders.

San Francisco and New York are already involved in counterintelligence actions and should continue to be alert for further opportunities. All other recipients should immediately devise at least two counterintelligence proposals and submit the same to the Bureau by 2/10/71. First proposal should be aimed strictly at creating dissension within the local branch. Second proposal should be aimed at creating dissension or problems between local branch and/or its leaders and BPP national headquarters. Submit each proposal in a separate airtel referencing this communication and in first paragraph specifically indicate whether the proposal is aimed at local dissension or national dissension.

In order for these proposals to be effective it is imperative that a close analysis be made of weaknesses and problems within the local BPP branch and that all proposals submitted be imaginative and timely. No proposal should be implemented without specific Bureau approval.

Source: Records of the Federal Bureau of Investigation, 1868–2008, Classification 157, Civil Unrest, Case Files, 1957–1978, Las Vegas, Nevada, 157-841. https://catalog. archives.gov/id/5255365. Accessed: January 24, 2017.

Airtel to Special Agent in Charge, Albany et al., from Director Federal Bureau of Investigation, March 1, 1971

Huey P. Newton expelled Eldridge Cleaver and the Algerian-based International Section of the BPP in February 1971. The expulsion demonstrates cleavages in the leadership of the BPP in the early 1970s. Newton wanted to focus primarily on creating economic opportunities and survival programs for black urban residents. Cleaver, who was in self-imposed exile in North Africa, supported a focus on revolutionary armed struggle against the U.S. government. Local branches and affiliates of the organization were forced to choose which leader they would follow. When branches decided to follow Cleaver, they were expelled from the party. Throughout the country members loyal to Cleaver attacked members loyal to Newton and members loyal to Newton attacked members loyal to Cleaver. The document below shows how the FBI wanted to use and exacerbate intraparty frictions to undermine the BPP.

Dissension between BPP Commander Huey P. Newton and Minister of Information Eldridge Cleaver in Algeria, which has been the objective of COINTELPRO, reached climax February twenty-six last when Cleaver publicly criticized actions of Newton and demanded demotion of Chief of Staff David Hilliard.

Newton and Hilliard on February twenty-seven last expelled Cleaver and entire international section.

February twenty-eight last BPP New York branches voted to disassociate with Newton-Hilliard led BPP and align with Eldridge Cleaver.

Recipients target informants and all sources to follow closely action of all BPP affiliated groups to determine who will remain loyal to Newton and who will align with Cleaver faction.

Follow closely and keep Bureau and San Francisco advised.

Source: https://catalog.archives/gov/id/5255365. Accessed January 4, 2017.

Memo to Special Agent in Charge, Albany et al., from Director Federal Bureau of Investigation, December 7, 1973

By 1973, there was growing suspicion among attorneys, journalists, and activists that the FBI had a secret counterintelligence program, which used questionable and even unconstitutional tactics to jail, discredit, and murder radical activists throughout the nation. As the document below shows, the growing clamor made by various groups led the FBI director to begin to address their secret program and attempt to justify its use. In the years

*and decades following this internal memo, legal actions by attorneys, jour-
nalists, and activists encouraged the federal government to release
confidential files that document the extensive, secret counterintelligence
program.*

RE memorandum to all special agents in charge 52-73, dated
11-27-73. With regard to news releases relating to the release of
Bureau documents to NBC newsman Carl Stern, I have issued the
following statement today. "As the result of a suit filed against the
FBI under the Freedom of Information Act, the Court has decided
that certain documents must be made public concerning a former
FBI program, which was known more commonly by its acronym,
'COINTELPRO-New Left.' These documents were released yester-
day to the plaintiff in the suit. Because of the misconceptions, misap-
prehensions, and false conclusions that could be drawn from partial
disclosure of this program, it is appropriate that I explain what the
program was about and why it was deemed necessary when it
was implemented in May 1968. In the late 1960's, a hard-core
revolutionary movement which came to be known as the 'New Left'
set out, in their own words to bring the government to its knees
through the use of force and violence. What started as the New Left
Movement chanting Marxist-Leninist slogans in the early years of
their 'revolution' developed into violent contempt, not only for
government and government officials, but for every responsible
American citizen. During these years, there were over 300 arsons or
attempted arsons, 14 destructive bombings, 9 persons killed, and
almost 600 injured on our college campuses alone. In the school year
1968-1969, damage of college campuses exceeded 3 million dollars
and in the next year mounted to an excess of 9.5 million. In this atmos-
phere of lawlessness in the cities mobs, overturned vehicles, set fires,
and damaged public and private property. There were threats to sabo-
tage power plants, to disrupt transportation and communications
facilities. Intelligence sources informed the FBI of plans that were discussed to poison public water supplies. At this time of national crisis,
the government would have been derelict in its duties had it not taken
measures to protect the fabric of our society. The FBI has the responsibility of investigating allegations of criminal violations and gather

intelligence regarding threats to the country's security. Because of the violent actions of the leadership of the New Left, FBI officials concluded that some additional effort must be made to neutralize and disrupt this revolutionary movement. This effort was called the 'Counterintelligence Program—New Left' or 'COINTELPRO-New Left.' While there is no way to measure the effect of the FBI's attempts at countersubversion, I believe that it did have some impact on the crisis at that time. Now, in the context of a different era where peace has returned to the college campuses and revolutionary forces no longer pose a major threat to peace and tranquility in our cities, some may deplore and condemn the FBI's use of a counterintelligence program —even against hostile and arrogant forces which openly sought to destroy this nation. I share the public's deep concern about citizen's rights to privacy and the preservation of all rights guaranteed under the Constitution and Bill of Rights. I have expressed this concern on several occasions since becoming director of the FBI. The acting Attorney General and I have discussed this situation, and we both agreed that an evaluation of FBI reactions in national security emergencies already under way should be continued. I plan to make a full report to the Attorney General. While such a counterintelligence program may not be the answer, there must be some effective way for the federal government to meet the challenge posed by those who will use any means to foment revolution. Mr. Bork and I both feel that perhaps additional legislation is required, and this is being given thorough study. We must carefully define FBI responsibilities and authority so that we can continue to fulfill the FBI's obligations to the citizens of the United States."

For your information the two documents released were Bureau memorandum to Albany, copies to all offices, dated 5-10-68, captioned "Counter Intelligence Program, Internal Security, Disruption of New Left"; and Bureau Airtel to SAC, Albany, copies to all offices, dates 4-28-71 captioned "Counter Intelligence Programs (COIN-TELPRO), Internal Security—Racial Matters," copies of which should be in our files. In the event you receive any inquiry concerning this matter you may release to the media copies of my statement as set forth above. However, you should not elaborate on this statement in any manner. Under no circumstances should you make available copies of the released documents. However, in the event you receive requests from any media representatives for copies of the released documents, you should refer them to FBI Headquarters.

Source: Records of the Federal Bureau of Investigation, 1868–2008, Classification 157, Civil Unrest, Case Files, 1957–1978, Las Vegas, Nevada, 157-841. https://catalog. Archives.gov/id/5255365. Accessed: January 4, 2017.

Bibliography

Abu-Jamal, Mumia. *We Want Freedom: A Life in the Black Panther Party.* Cambridge, MA: South End Press, 2004.

Alkebulan, Paul. *Survival Pending Revolution: The History of the Black Panther Party.* Tuscaloosa: University of Alabama Press, 2007.

Anthony, Earl. *Picking Up the Gun: A Report on the Black Panthers.* New York: Dial Press, 1970.

Araiza, Lauren. " 'In Common Struggle against a Common Oppression': The United Farm Workers and the Black Panther Party, 1968–1973." *The Journal of African American History* 94, no. 2 (2009): 200–23. http://www.jstor.org/stable/25610076.

Austin, Curtis J. *Up Against the Wall: Violence and the Making and Unmaking of the Black Panther Party.* Fayetteville: University of Arkansas Press, 2006.

Bass, Paul, and Douglas W. Rae. *Murder in the Model City: The Black Panthers, Yale, and the Redemption of a Killer.* New York: Basic Books, 2006.

Bingham, Howard L. *Howard L. Bingham's Black Panthers, 1968.* Los Angeles: Ammo, 2009.

Bloom, Joshua, and Martin Waldo E. *Black against Empire: The History and Politics of the Black Panther Party.* Berkeley: University of California Press, 2013.

Boykoff, Jules, and Martha Gies. " 'We're Going to Defend Ourselves': The Portland Chapter of the Black Panther Party and the Local Media Response." *Oregon Historical Quarterly* 111, no. 3 (2010): 278–311. doi:10.5403/oregonhistq .111.3.0278.

Brent, William Lee. *Long Time Gone: A Black Panther's True-Life Story of His Skyjacking and Twenty-Five Years in Cuba.* New York: Times Books, 1996.

Brown, Elaine. *A Taste of Power: A Black Woman's Story.* New York: Pantheon Books, 1992.

Brown, Scot. *Fighting for Us: Maulana Karenga, the US Organization, and Black Cultural Nationalism.* New York: New York University Press, 2003.

Bukari, Safiya, and Laura Whitehorn. *The War Before: The True Life Story of Becoming a Black Panther, Keeping the Faith in Prison and Fighting for Those Left Behind.* New York: Feminist Press at the City University of New York, 2010.

Bullins, Ed. "Who He Is Now: Ed Bullins Replies." *Black American Literature Forum* 13, no. 3 (1979): 109. doi:10.2307/3041526.

Calloway, Carolyn R. "Group Cohesiveness in the Black Panther Party." *Journal of Black Studies* 8, no. 1 (1977): 55–74. http://www.jstor.org/stable/2783689.

Churchill, Ward. *Agents of Repression: The FBI's Secret War against the Black Panther Party and the American Indian Movement.* Boston: South End Press, 1988.

Churchill, Ward. *To Disrupt, Discredit and Destroy: The FBI's Secret War against the Panther Party.* New York: Routledge, 2009.

Cleaver, Eldridge, and Henry Louis Gates. "Eldridge Cleaver on Ice." *Transition,* no. 75/76 (1997): 294–311. doi:10.2307/2935422.

Cleaver, Kathleen Neal, and Susie Linfield. "The Education of Kathleen Neal Cleaver." *Transition,* no. 77 (1998): 172–95. doi:10.2307/2903207.

Cleaver, Kathleen, and George Katsiaficas, eds. *Liberation, Imagination, and the Black Panther Party.* New York: Routledge, 2001.

Cleaver, Kathleen, ed. *Target Zero: Life in Writing.* New York: Palgrave Macmillan, 2006.

Collier-Thomas, Bettye, and V. P. Franklin. *Sisters in Struggle: African American Women in the Civil Rights—Black Power Movement.* New York: New York University Press, 2001.

Conway, Marshall, and Dominique Stevenson. *Marshall Law: The Life and Times of a Baltimore Black Panther.* Oakland: AK Press, 2011.

Courtright, John A. "Rhetoric of the Gun: An Analysis of the Rhetorical Modifications of the Black Panther Party." *Journal of Black Studies* 4, no. 3 (1974): 249–67. http://www.jstor.org/stable/2783656.

Crowe, Daniel Edward. *Prophets of Rage: The Black Freedom Struggle in San Francisco, 1945–1969.* New York: Garland, 2000.

Davenport, Christian. *Media Bias, Perspective, and State Repression: The Black Panther Party.* Cambridge: Cambridge University Press, 2010.

Dixon, Aaron. *My People Rising: Memoir of a Black Panther Captain.* Chicago: Haymarket Books, 2012.

Douglas, Emory, Bobby Seale, Sam Durant, and Sonia Sanchez. *Black Panther: The Revolutionary Art of Emory Douglas.* New York: Rizzoli, 2007.

Fanon, Frantz. *Toward the African Revolution:* New York: Grove Press, 1967.

Foner, Philip S., ed. *The Black Panthers Speak: The Manifesto of the Party. The First Complete Documentary Record of the Panthers' Program.* New York: Da Capo Press, 1995.

Franklin, V. P. "Jackanapes: Reflections on the Legacy of the Black Panther Party for the Hip Hop Generation." *The Journal of African American History* 92, no. 4 (2007): 553–60. http://www.jstor.org/stable/20064233.

Freed, Donald. *Agony in New Haven: The Trial of Bobby Seale Ericka Huggins and the Black Panther Party.* New York: Simon and Schuster, 1973.

Fujino, Diane. *Samurai among Panthers: Richard Aoki on Race, Resistance, and a Paradoxical Life.* Minneapolis: University of Minnesota Press, 2012.

Gore, Dayo F., Jeanne Theoharis, and Komozi Wood. *Want to Start a Revolution? Radical Women in the Black Freedom Struggle.* New York: New York University Press, 2009.

Haas, Jeffrey. *The Assassination of Fred Hampton.* Chicago: Lawrence Hill Books, 2010.

Haines, Herbert H. *Black Radicals and the Civil Rights Mainstream, 1954–1970.* Knoxville: University of Tennessee Press, 1988.

Harper, Frederick D. "The Influence of Malcolm X on Black Militancy." *Journal of Black Studies* 1, no. 4 (1971): 387–402. http://www.jstor.org/stable/2783817.

Harris, Jessica C. "Revolutionary Black Nationalism." *Journal of Negro History* 86 (2001): 409–21.

Haskins, James. *Power to the People: The Rise and Fall of the Black Panther Party.* New York: Simon and Schuster Books for Young Readers, 1997.

Heath, G. Louis, ed. *The Black Panther Leaders Speak: Huey P. Newton, Bobby Seale, Eldridge Cleaver and Company Speak Out through the Black Panther Party's Official Newspaper.* Metuchen, NJ: Scarecrow Press, 1976.

Henderson, Errol A. "The Lumpenproletariat as Vanguard?: The Black Panther Party, Social Transformation, and Pearson's Analysis of Huey Newton." *Journal of Black Studies* 28, no. 2 (1997): 171–99. http://www.jstor.org/stable/2784850.

Heynen, Nik. "Bending the Bars of Empire from Every Ghetto for Survival: The Black Panther Party's Radical Antihunger Politics of Social Reproduction and Scale." *Annals of the Association of American Geographers* 99, no. 2 (2009): 406–22. http://www.jstor.org/stable/25515206.

Hilliard, David, and Lewis Cole. *This Side of Glory.* Boston: Little, Brown and Company, 1993.

Hilliard, David, ed. *The Black Panther: Intercommunal News Service, 1967–1980.* New York: Atria, 2007.

Hilliard, David. *The Black Panther Party: Service to the People Program.* Albuquerque: University of New Mexico Press, 2008.

Hilliard, David, Keith Zimmerman, and Kent Zimmerman. *Huey: Spirit of the Panther.* New York: Thunder's Mouth Press, 2006.

Hind, Robert J. "The Internal Colonial Concept." *Comparative Studies in Society and History* 26, no. 3 (1984): 543–68. http://www.jstor.org/stable/178555.

Höhn, Maria. "The Black Panther Solidarity Committees and the Voice of the Lumpen." *German Studies Review* 31, no. 1 (2008): 133–54. http://www.jstor.org/stable/27668453.

Jeffries, Hasan Kwame. *Bloody Lowndes: Civil Rights and Black Power in Alabama's Black Belt.* New York: New York University Press, 2009.

Jeffries, Judson L. *Huey P. Newton: The Radical Theorist.* Jackson: University Press of Mississippi, 2002.

Jeffries, Judson L., ed. *Comrades. A Local History of the Black Panther Party.* Bloomington: Indiana University Press, 2007.

Jeffries, Judson L., ed. *On the Ground: The Black Panther Party in Communities across America.* Jackson: University of Mississippi Press, 2010.

Jennings, Regina. "Poetry of the Black Panther Party: Metaphors of Militancy." *Journal of Black Studies* 29, no. 1 (1998): 106–29. http://www.jstor.org/stable/2668059.

Jones, Charles E., ed. *The Black Panther Party (Reconsidered)*. Baltimore: Black Classic Press, 1998.

Jones, Charles E. "The Political Repression of the Black Panther Party 1966–1971: The Case of the Oakland Bay Area." *Journal of Black Studies* 18, no. 4 (1988): 415–34. http://www.jstor.org/stable/2784371.

Joseph, Jamal. *Panther Baby: A Life of Rebellion and Reinvention*. Chapel Hill, NC: Algonquin Books, 2012.

Joseph, Peniel E. *The Black Power Movement: Rethinking the Civil Rights–Black Power Era*. New York: Routledge, 2006.

Joseph, Peniel. *Waiting 'Til the Midnight Hour: A Narrative History of Black Power in America*. New York: Henry Holt and Company, 2006.

Joseph, Peniel E. "The Black Power Movement: A State of the Field." *The Journal of American History* 96, no. 3 (2009): 751–76. http://www.jstor.org/stable/25622477.

Killian, Lewis M. *The Impossible Revolution? Black Power and the American Dream*. New York: Random House, 1968.

King, Robert Hillary. *From the Bottom of the Heap: The Autobiography of Black Panther Robert Hillary King*. Oakland, CA: PM Press 2009.

Lockwood, Lee. *Conversations with Eldridge Cleaver: Algiers, New York*. New York: McGraw Hill, 1970.

Lothian, Kathy. "Seizing the Time: Australian Aborigines and the Influence of the Black Panther Party, 1969–1972." *Journal of Black Studies* 35, no. 4 (2005): 179–200. http://www.jstor.org/stable/40027217.

Major, Reginald. *A Panther Is a Black Cat*. Baltimore: Black Classic Press, 2006.

Martine, Gene. *The Black Panthers*. New York: Signet Books. 1969.

McCartney, John T. *Black Power Ideologies: An Essay in African American Political Thought*. Philadelphia: Temple University Press, 1992.

McCutchen, Steve. *We Are Free for a While: Back to Back in the Black Panther Party*. Baltimore: PublishAmerica, 2008.

Meier, August, Elliot Rudwick, and John Bracey Jr., eds. *Black Protest in the Sixties*. Princeton, NJ: Marcus Wiener, 1991.

Morris, Aldon D. *The Origins of the Civil Rights Movement*. New York: Free Press, 1984.

Murch, Donna. *Living for the City: Migration, Education, and the Rise of the Black Panther Party in Oakland, California.* Chapel Hill: The University of North Carolina Press, 2010.

Nelson, Alondra. *Body and Soul: The Black Panther Party and the Fight against Medical Discrimination.* Minneapolis and London: University of Minnesota Press, 2010.

Newton, Huey P. *To Die for the People: The Writing of Huey P. Newton.* New York: Vintage Books, 1972.

Newton, Huey P. *Revolutionary Suicide.* New York: Harcourt Brace Jovanovich, 1973.

Newton, Huey P. *War against the Panthers: A Study of Repression in America.* New York: Harlem River Press, 1996.

Newton, Huey P., David Hilliard, Donald Weis, and Frederika Newton. *The Huey P. Newton Reader.* New York: Seven Stories Press, 2003.

Newton, Michael. *Bitter Grain: Huey Newton and the Black Panther Party.* Los Angeles: Holloway House, 1980.

Ngozi-Brown, Scot. "The US Organization, Maulana Karenga, and Conflict with the Black Panther Party: A Critique of Sectarian Influences on Historical Discourse." *Journal of Black Studies* 28, no. 2 (1997): 157–70. http://www.jstor.org/stable/2784849.

Ogbar, Jeffrey O. G. *Black Power: Radical Politics and African American Identity.* Baltimore: Johns Hopkins University Press, 2004.

Olsen, Jack. *Last Man Standing: The Tragedy and Triumph of Geronimo Pratt.* New York: Doubleday, 2000.

Ongiri, Amy Abugo. "Prisoner of Love: Affiliation, Sexuality, and the Black Panther Party." *The Journal of African American History* 94, no. 1 (2009): 69–86. http://www.jstor.org/stable/25610049.

O'Reilly, Kenneth. *Racial Matters: The FBI's Secret File on Black America, 1960–1972.* New York: Free Press, 1989.

Pearson, Hugh. *The Shadow of the Panther: Huey P. Newton and the Price of Black Power in America.* Boston: Addison-Wesley, 1994.

Pharr, Wayne. *Nine Lives of a Black Panther.* Chicago: Lawrence Hill Books, 2014.

Reed, Adolph L. "Strategy for a Communist Agenda: Civil Rights Equals Social Revolution." *Phylon (1960-)* 37, no. 4 (1976): 334–42. doi:10.2307/274497

Rhodes, Jane. *Framing the Black Panthers: The Spectacular Rise of a Black Power Icon.* New York: New Press, 2007.

Rhomberg, Chris. *No There There: Race, Class, and Political Community in Oakland.* Berkeley: University of California Press, 2004.

Robinson, Cedric J. *Black Marxism: The Making of the Black Radical Tradition.* London: Zed Books, 1983.

Sandarg, Robert. "Jean Genet and the Black Panther Party." *Journal of Black Studies* 16, no. 3 (1986): 269–82. http://www.jstor.org/stable/2784171.

Schanche, Don. *The Panther Paradox: A Liberal's Dilemma.* New York: David McKay, 1970.

Scheer, Robert, ed. *Eldridge Cleaver: Post Prison Writings and Speeches.* New York: Vintage Books, 1967.

Seale, Bobby. *Seize the Time: The Story of the Black Panther Party and Huey P. Newton.* New York: Random House, 1970.

Seale, Bobby. *A Lonely Rage: The Autobiography of Bobby Seale.* New York: Times Books, 1978.

Self, Robert O. *American Babylon: Race and the Struggle for Postwar Oakland.* Princeton, NJ: Princeton University Press, 2003.

Shakur, Assata. *Assata: An Autobiography.* Chicago: Lawrence Hill Books, 1987.

Shames, Stephen, and Charles Jones. *The Black Panthers.* New York: Aperture Foundation, 2006.

Sheehy, Gail. *Panthermania: The Clash of Black against Black in One American City.* New York: Harper and Row, 1971.

Shih, Bryan, and Yohuru Williams. *The Black Panthers: Portraits from an Unfinished Revolution.* New York: Nation Books, 2016.

Singh, Nikhil Pal. *Black Is a Country: Race and the Unfinished Struggle for Democracy.* Cambridge: Harvard University Press, 2004.

Slate, Nico. *Black Power beyond Borders: The Global Dimensions of the Black Power Movement.* New York: Palgrave Macmillan, 2012.

Smith, Jennifer B. *An International History of the Black Panther Party.* New York: Garland, 1999.

Spencer, Robyn. *The Revolution Has Come: Black Power, Gender, and the Black Panther Party in Oakland.* Durham and London: Duke University Press. 2016.

Tyner, James A. " 'Defend the Ghetto': Space and the Urban Politics of the Black Panther Party." *Annals of the Association of American Geographers* 96, no. 1 (2006): 105–18. http://www.jstor.org/stable/3694147.

Van Deburg, William L. *New Day in Babylon: The Black Power Movement in American Culture, 1965–1975.* Chicago: University of Chicago Press, 1997.

Van Peebles, Mario, Ula Y. Taylor, and J. Tarika Lewis. *Panther: A Pictorial History of the Black Panthers and the Story behind the Film.* New York: New Market Press, 1995.

Williams, Jakobi. " 'Don't No Woman Have to Do Nothing She Don't Want to Do': Gender, Activism, and the Illinois Black Panther Party." *Black Women, Gender Families* 6, no. 2 (2012): 29–54. doi:10.5406/blacwomegendfami.6.2.0029.

Williams, Jakobi. *From the Bullet to the Ballot: The Illinois Chapter of the Black Panther Party and Racial Coalition Politics in Chicago.* Chapel Hill: The University of North Carolina Press, 2013.

Williams, Yohuru. *Black Politics/White Power: Civil Rights, Black Power, and the Black Panthers in New Haven.* St. James, New York: Brandywine Press, 2000.

Williams, Yohuru, and Jama Lazerow, eds. *In Search of the Black Panther Party: New Perspectives on a Revolutionary Moment.* Durham and London: Duke University Press, 2007.

Williams, Yohuru, and Jama Lazerow, eds. *Liberated Territory: Untold Local Perspectives of the Black Panther Party.* Durham and London: Duke University Press, 2008.

Williams, Yohuru. " 'Some Abstract Thing Called Freedom': Civil Rights, Black Power, and the Legacy of the Black Panther Party." *OAH Magazine of History* 22, no. 3 (2008): 16–21. http://www.jstor.org/stable/25162181.

Wilson, Jamie J. *The Black Panther Party of Connecticut.* New Haven, CT: Amistad Committee, Inc., 2014.

Wilson, Jamie J. *Civil Rights Movement.* Santa Barbara: Greenwood, 2013.

Index

About the Author

JAMIE J. WILSON is a professor of history at Salem State University in Massachusetts. His work has appeared in the *International Social Science Review*, *Biography*, and *Afro Americans in New York Life and History*. He is also the author of *Building a Healthy Black Harlem* (2009), *Civil Rights Movement* (2013), and *The Black Panther Party of Connecticut* (2014).

Printed in the USA
CPSIA information can be obtained
at www.ICGtesting.com
LVHW010834201223
766775LV00006B/277